Black Sea

Çay

Samsun ○

Dundartepe

(Nerik?)   Merzifon (Hattena?)

Gumushacıkoy   • Horoztepe
(Hanhana?)   ◉ Amasya (Hakpis?)

Alaca H.   Turhal (Gaziura)   Yeşil Irmak   K   Çay

ılıkaya   • Eskiyapar

• Boğazköy   Sivas ◉ (Marassantiya?)
(Hattusas)

Divriği ◉ (Samuha?)
• Alışar   • (Kussara?)

• Kültepe (Kanesh)

Elâziğ ○

emköy   Kayseri ○

Fraktin •   Malatya ◉
(Tegarama?)

Elbistan ◉
(Lawazantiya?)

Şar ◉ (Kummani?)

Ceyhan

Seyhan

• İvriz   • Gedikli
• Karatepe
Adana (Adaniya)   ◉ İslâhiye
Tarsus ◉   • Sirkeli   • Yesemek   Jera ◉
lersin ◉

Meydancık (Datassa?)

Tell Atchana (Alalah)

Aleppo ◉
(Halpa)

Orontes   Firat (Euphrates)

Ras •
Shamra (Ugarit)

0   50   100km.

Ancient Peoples and Places

THE HITTITES

General Editor

PROFESSOR GLYN DANIEL

ABOUT THE AUTHOR

J. G. Macqueen was born in Glasgow in 1932, and educated at Hutchesons' Boys'
Grammar School, St Andrews University and Magdalen College, Oxford. In
1957 he was Scholar of the British Institute of Archaeology at Ankara, and after
National Service in the Royal Engineers he was appointed to the staff of the
Department of Classics at Bristol University, where he is now Senior Lecturer.
His principal research work has been in Anatolian languages, religion and
historical geography, and he has excavated and done field-survey work in Turkey.
He has also written a book on the history and civilization of ancient Babylon.

THE
HITTITES
AND THEIR CONTEMPORARIES IN ASIA MINOR

J. G. Macqueen

68 PHOTOGRAPHS
61 LINE DRAWINGS
2 MAPS

Westview Press · Boulder, Colorado

THIS IS VOLUME EIGHTY-THREE IN THE SERIES
Ancient Peoples and Places
GENERAL EDITOR: PROFESSOR GLYN DANIEL

/

Published 1975 in the United States of America by
  Westview Press, Inc.
  1898 Flatiron Court
  Boulder, Colorado 80301
  Frederick A. Praeger, Publisher and Editorial Director

First published 1975 in London, England
by Thames and Hudson Ltd.

Library of Congress Cataloging in Publication Data

Macqueen, James G.
  The Hittites and their contemporaries in Asia Minor.

  (Ancient peoples and places; v. 83)
  Bibliography: p.
  Includes index.
    1. Hittites. 2. Asia Minor—Civilization.
  I. Title.
  DS66.M23   1975   939.2   75-26838
  ISBN 0-89158-520-6

Printed in the United States of America

CONTENTS

List of Illustrations

Preface

Research on the Hittite period in Anatolia has expanded greatly in recent years. While 'traditional' sites such as Boğazköy continue to produce their annual quota of exciting material, investigations at other central Anatolian sites (Inandik, Eskiyapar) are revealing new aspects of Hittite culture; at the same time excavations in other areas are constantly adding to our knowledge and altering our perspectives. In the south-east (Korucutepe, Norşuntepe), the west (Miletus, Aphrodisias), and most recently the north (Maşat, the Samsun-Bafra area) and the south (Meydancik Kalesi in Cilicia Tracheia) the picture is changing even more rapidly. Is this then, it may be asked, a good time to publish a book about the Hittites and their contemporaries? The answer, surely, is that any book on this topic is at most an account of work in progress, and I hope that this one will be accepted as such.

My aim has been to combine textual and archaeological evidence in a single narrative. I am fully aware of the dangers involved in riding this academic tandem, but I feel that the attempt must be made in order to present an all-round picture of life in Late Bronze Age Anatolia.

I am most grateful to Professor Glyn Daniel for inviting me to contribute this book to the 'Ancient Peoples and Places' series, and wish to thank Professor J. M. Cook, Professor O. R. Gurney, Mr James Mellaart and others too numerous to mention for provision and discussion of information; Mrs Janet Gliddon, Mrs Jeanne Bishop and Miss Rachel Lee for their faultless typing; Mr Gordon Kelsey and Mr Martyn Williams for their invaluable help with the photographs; and most of all my wife, not only for her illustrations but also for her support and encouragement throughout an over-lengthy period of literary gestation. I dedicate this book to her.

J.G.M.

CHAPTER I

Background and Environment

The area which we know as Anatolia or Asia Minor is part of the great mountain-system which extends from beyond the Himalayas to the Atlantic seaboard of France, Spain and North Africa. It consists of a high central plateau of ancient rock averaging about three thousand feet above sea-level, and limited to north and south by the geologically newer folds of the Pontus and Taurus Mountains. The whole forms a huge peninsula thrusting out between the Black Sea and the Mediterranean, and sloping gradually down from the Armenian mountains in the east until its rocky ridges extend out into and finally disappear under the waters of the Aegean Sea.

Fig. 1

Bordering as it does on Syria and Mesopotamia to the south-east, and on Europe to the north-west, Anatolia has inevitably been an area which has seen many incursions of peoples and many changes of government. But it would be wrong to think of it merely as a 'land-bridge' between Asia and Europe. The peoples who were attracted to Anatolia did not come merely because it was a convenient short-cut, but because it was a land of rich possibilities, a source of important raw materials and a primary centre rather than a peripheral backwater which served only to link more favoured areas. This is the case not only in the later second millennium, which will be our main concern in the present volume, but in many other periods of its long history. Ionia, for instance, was the area in which what we think of as Greek civilization first grew up. For the Romans, the province of Asia was one of the richest of their empire, and ultimately they recognized that the centre of political, cultural and economic gravity was far to the east of Italy, and moved their capital to Constantinople, a city which, though not actually in Anatolia, is only a mile or two away across the straits.

What was the attraction of Anatolia? It was, first of all, a rich source of timber and agricultural products of all kinds. This is difficult to believe when one looks at the arid, treeless steppe-country of central Anatolia today, but the more fertile coastal regions and the sheltered

Plate 1

9

Fig. 1 Map of present-day Anatolia

valleys of the interior give some idea of what much of the country must have been like before the destruction of trees by goats and timber-hungry humans, followed by centuries of neglect, reduced it to its present state. Certainly the presence of large and numerous ancient settlements in areas such as that to the south of the central Salt Lake which are now semi-desert, is an indication that conditions were very different in ancient times.

But agricultural wealth alone cannot account for the attraction of Anatolia. It was no more fertile than other areas whose inhabitants were drawn towards it. What they were looking for, and what Anatolia could provide for them, was an abundance of the mineral wealth which with the advance of civilization became increasingly necessary. The mountains of Anatolia are rich in metal-deposits, and it will be seen in the course of our narrative how important metalliferous areas were in the political and economic history of the Middle East.

In the last few years it has become clear that even in the Neolithic period, before the development of metalworking, Anatolia was an area of vital importance in human development. The discovery that animals and crops could be domesticated, which was first made in the Middle East between 9000 and 7000 BC, has been described as a 'Neolithic Revolution', but its importance lies not so much in its immediate effect (the establishment of settled agricultural villages) as in its enormous potential as a basis for further advance, given the right stimulus and the right conditions. An agricultural village does not grow automatically into a town, but one result of its formation is an increased demand for materials, such as flint and obsidian, which are necessary to make cultivating tools and other equipment. At the same time it makes its inhabitants much less mobile than their hunting forbears, and so less able to find these materials for themselves. In this way trade becomes increasingly important, and those communities which happen to have vital materials on their doorsteps are in a position which they can exploit to the full. Such communities can rapidly increase in wealth and in size, for agriculture provides not only the stimulus for their advance but also the economic basis on which it can be founded. It need hardly be added that this is not the only way in which communities can increase – in southern Mesopotamia, for instance, a main stimulus appears to have been a lack of raw materials rather than a monopoly of

Fig. 2 Wall-painting from Çatal Hüyük, perhaps showing volcanic eruption with town in foreground. c. *6200* BC *(after Mellaart)*

them – but a community of the type described has recently been discovered at Çatal Hüyük in the Konya Plain in southern Anatolia. This Neolithic town covers an area of 32 acres, and is by far the largest site of its age so far found. It was occupied from before 7000 BC until about 5600 BC, and it is reasonably assumed that its precocious development was based not only on an agricultural and pastoral economy, made possible by the ideal conditions offered by the gradual drying-up of a Pluvial lake in what is now the Konya Plain, but also on the community's control of the obsidian which was obtained from the near-by volcanoes of the Hasan Dağ and Karaca Dağ. An interesting wall-painting which has been preserved has been interpreted by the excavator as a view of the town with an eruption of Hasan Dağ in the background. More recent exploration has shown the presence of Neolithic remains, earlier than those of Çatal Hüyük and clearly connected with obsidian-working, at sites nearer Hasan Dağ, and it is possible that further sites like Çatal Hüyük will be found in other obsidian-producing areas – eastern Anatolia, for instance – if the agricultural potential proves to have been sufficiently high to support them. No such sites are yet known, but there is evidence for the export of eastern Anatolian obsidian to the 'Zagros area, on the borders of Iraq and Iran, as early as c. 30,000 BC.

Fig. 2

Though their prosperity was based on obsidian, the inhabitants of Çatal Hüyük were also acquainted with the use of other local materials which were to be of infinitely greater value in the later history of Anatolia. Already before 7000 BC at Çayönü, close to the rich Ergani Maden copper⁄mines near modern Elazığ, native copper was being shaped into tools and pins, and before 6000 BC local smiths at Çatal Hüyük had mastered the technique of smelting, and were producing copper and lead beads and other small trinkets. Slowly methods of production and workmanship were improved, and the use of metal spread from its original mountain home (or homes: other areas, such as Iran, must have had an equal part to play) into the plains of Mesopotamia, where metal⁄working was introduced before 5000 BC as a feature of the Tell Halaf culture, a culture which is in many ways strongly reminiscent of Anatolia.[1] From this time on, the Anatolian mountains were always a principal source of metals and of metallurgical techniques to the Mesopotamian world.

It is unfortunate that developments in metallurgy are so often difficult to follow because of lack of evidence. Unlike scrap pottery, scrap metal can be, and normally is, melted down for re⁄use, and it is only by chance that specimens survive. Often the only way in which one can tell what the metal vessels of a particular period looked like is to study the shapes of the pottery which was made and even coloured to imitate metal. In a few instances the discovery of 'royal' tombs in which metal vessels and implements are preserved yields information of far greater value than that of the gold and silver found. But such tombs as have so far been discovered date from a much later period.

With the increased importance of metals and metal technology, the north⁄central and north⁄western parts of Anatolia, which contained rich metal⁄deposits, were increasingly developed, and settlements began to grow and prosper. But it is worthwhile mentioning that they grew in their own characteristic way, quite unlike that of areas such as Egypt and Mesopotamia where conditions and stimuli were different. In southern Mesopotamia for instance the settlements grew up around temples, and the temple with its lofty tower became a central feature.[2] But in Anatolia we can glimpse something else happening. The best illustration of this is perhaps the little settlement of Hacılar in the 'Lake District' of southern Turkey. In the years before about 5400 BC Hacılar had, apart from an attractive pottery⁄style, little to distin⁄guish it from other contemporary agricultural villages in the Middle East. But about 5400 a rectangular area measuring 190 by 120 feet was cut off and fortified by an enclosure wall of mud brick. Inside this

Fig. 3

unexcavated area

Fig. 3 Isometric view of Hacılar II–I, c. 5400–5250 BC: c courtyard; g granary; gr guardroom; p potters' workshops; w well; s shrine (after Mellaart)

fortification were a granary, potters' workshops, a well and a small shrine. Clearly the local ruler had constructed a rudimentary fortress for the safety and comfort of himself and his followers. After the destruction of this castle another larger one was built on the same site, and it is possible to see in these structures the beginning of something that was to be characteristic of the Anatolian-Aegean area at a later period – the fortified citadel. The outline of the development can be seen in what looks like a section of a similar structure at Can Hasan, just north of the Taurus, and then at Mersin in Cilicia, where one can see the rooms inside the wall with their slit-windows overlooking the country below, the piles of sling-stones made ready for action, and the 'commander's residence' alongside the narrow entrance. Later still, in the third millenium BC, the fortified citadel can be seen in both central and western Anatolia. The same essential pattern is to be found in Greece as early as about 3000 BC, at the site of Dimini in Thessaly. Its survival in the

Fig. 4

Fig. 5

15

Fig. 4 Isometric view of
Mersin XVI citadel,
c. 4000 BC (after Lloyd)

Fig. 5 Reconstructed plan of
Troy II citadel, c. 2300
BC (after Lloyd)

0   5
m.

0   10   20   30   40   50
m.

citadels of Mycenaean and Classical Greece, and its ultimate introduction by the Crusaders to western Europe, are subjects which are beyond
the scope of this book.

To return to Anatolia, the area seems by the latter part of the third
millennium BC to have become a land of small city-states, their rulers
living in castles, their economies based primarily on agriculture, but
their real wealth and importance residing in their metals and metal
products. Examples of these products are to be seen in the 'treasures' of
Alaca Hüyük and other sites in north-central Anatolia, and of Troy in   *Fig. 6*
the north-west. Similar finds have also been reported from Dorak near
Lake Apolyont, and doubtless others will turn up in the future. These
treasures are of comparatively late date (say 2300 BC for Troy and 2200
for Alaca), but the advanced nature of the techniques employed makes
it certain that they are the products of a long tradition of metalworking.
Although their relationship to the equally famous treasures of Maikop,   *Fig. 7*
north of the Caucasus,[3] and Ur in southern Mseopotamia[4] has yet
to be fully worked out, it can be claimed that the Anatolian works are
not mere derivatives from another area – certainly not from the more
'civilized' south-east. There has in fact been a feeling among some
Mesopotamian archaeologists that the Ur treasures are intrusive here,
brought by some foreign dynasty from the north. This would certainly
been in keeping with the earlier patterns of influence noted above.

Fig. 6 Bull-figure from Alaca, c. 2200 BC

Fig. 7 Bull-figure from Maikop, c. 2200 BC

Fig. 8 Fragment of gold overlay from a piece of furniture, with cartouche of the Fifth Dynasty pharaoh Sahure (c. 2475 BC). Said to be from a tomb at Dorak (after Lloyd)

Fig. 8

So Anatolia in the period (*c.* 2600–2300 BC) which is known to archaeologists as 'Early Bronze II' was in a commanding position. It had both the resources that were necessary for a Bronze Age economy and the techniques needed to exploit them. Thus, it had an important part to play in the Middle Eastern world, and its connections spread out as far as southern Mesopotamia (Ur) and Egypt (if we accept the evidence from Dorak). To the metal-less rulers of Mesopotamia it must have been of particular importance, and so we find it included in the many areas to which they dispatched their merchants. Legend (though not yet archaeology) tells of the activities of merchants sent out about 2300 BC by the kings of Akkad to the town of Purushanda, which probably lay south of the central Salt Lake or in the Konya Plain. Partial confirmation of the existence of this trade is to be found at the site of Tell Brak,[5] on the caravan-route from northern Mesopotamia to Anatolia, where Naram-Sin of Akkad built an elaborate palace in the ruins of which were discovered several imports from Anatolia.

The destruction of the empire of Akkad by barbarian invasions led to the interruption of this trade, but by about 1940 BC merchants from Assyria were to be found at several towns in Anatolia, notably at Kanesh near modern Kayseri, where extensive excavations in the *karum* or trading-quarter have revealed not only the houses of these merchants but also large quantities of their business correspondence written on tablets of clay. From these records we can see what the principal articles of trade were, and perhaps deduce both the importance of Anatolia at the time and the difficulties that were to influence political policy throughout the second millennium. The Assyrians clearly wanted silver, gold and copper, and what they gave in exchange was woolen cloth, made-up clothing of various types, and a metal which despite much argument is almost certainly tin rather than lead. In this trade we can see both the reasons for the prosperity of the Anatolians and the principal difficulty they had in maintaining that prosperity. For Anatolia, although it is rich in minerals and has plentiful supplies of copper, is comparatively poor in tin. There are some small deposits, but nothing like enough to supply the needs of a full Bronze Age economy. Where the Assyrians got their tin from is not quite clear, but it was probably from the hills east and north of their homeland. At any rate the Anatolians were eager to have it. So a largely peaceful relationship developed between the local communities and the Assyrian merchants, who lived in Anatolian houses, used Anatolian equipment, and often, if we can trust the evidence of proper names, took Anatolian wives. In fact, were it not for the language of the documents it would often be impossible to detect 'Assyrian' influence at all, and some of the best evidence for one of the richest and finest' periods of Anatolian crafts-manship is to be found in the houses of the Assyrian merchants. Other sites, such as Hattus at modern Boğazköy, Acemköy near Aksaray, and Karahüyük near Konya also attest the prosperity of central Anatolia at this time. In the south-west too there are signs of equal prosperity at Beycesultan, where a large palace and other public buildings on a grand scale have been excavated, while in the north-west Troy was beginning to recover from a period of comparative decline and would soon take its place once more as an important site. These areas too presumably had their sources of tin (other metals were amply available), but it is at present not clear what they were. A possible source will be suggested below.

About 1780 BC, for reasons which are not yet completely clear but which are probably connected with political and ethnic movements in Mesopotamia, the Assyrian trade-connection with central Anatolia

Figs. 9, 10

Fig. 9 Ritual vase in form of a lion: from Kültepe

Fig. 10 Beak-spouted vessel from the Assyrian merchant colony at Boğazköy/Hattusas. H. 16 in.

came to an abrupt end. The Hurrians, a people of unknown affiliations whose original homeland seems to have been in the region of Lake Urmia and who had for many years been spreading across northern Mesopotamia towards the Mediterranean Sea, had by now begun to achieve political supremacy in the states on the upper Tigris and Euphrates and in the hills bordering on south-east Anatolia. This meant that Assyria was cut off from her commercial colonies, and her power quickly collapsed. Soon she was incorporated into the expanding empire of Hammurabi of Babylon.

For the Anatolians, the loss of their tin-supplies was a disastrous blow. On the whole, the cities that flourished during the period of the Assyrian merchant-colonies went into a decline from which they never recovered, and as Hurrian pressure built up to the east the situation grew more serious. Not only Assyria, but the routes through the Anti-Taurus were lost. The only alternative was the one running down through Cilicia, across to the Euphrates, and on to southern Mesopotamia. That this too was a tin-route, and that it had connections with Kanesh, can be seen from the archives of Mari on the middle Euphrates. The trouble with this route was that it was in the hands of powerful kingdoms – Babylon in the south, Mari in the centre, and Aleppo in the north. Yet tin there had to be, and inevitably the interests of the central Anatolians were drawn towards the Euphrates-route and the dangerous ground of Middle Eastern politics.

During the last years of the Assyrian trading-colonies the dominating position in central Anatolian affairs had been seized by the rulers of the state of Kussara, a city which is often said to have been in central Anatolia, but which was more probably situated further to the east, in the area around modern Divriği, near one of the routes from Assyria. Pithanas, the first recorded ruler of this state, extended his influence to Nesas, which may well be an alternative spelling of Kanesh in an attempt to represent an original Knesh (developing in the same way as the English knee) with the addition of a nominal suffix -as. His son Anittas extended his conquests to other central Anatolian principalities including Hattus, which he destroyed and declared accursed, and by the end of his life (c. 1750 BC) he had acquired a sufficiently substantial kingdom to claim the title of 'great king'. Unfortunately our documentary evidence fails us at this point, and it is impossible to say what happened to the kingdom of Anittas. In a large burnt building at Kanesh a spearhead has been discovered bearing the inscription 'palace of Anita, the king', and the building may also, for all we know, have contained the burnt remains of its ruler. Who the destroyers were is unknown, but when the picture becomes clearer again, about a hundred years later, we find a ruler who claims that his origin is in Kussara setting up his capital at Hattus (or Hattusas as it is now called), and to celebrate the event changing his name to Hattusilis. Whatever his connection with the earlier rulers – and in view of his flouting of the curse it may not have been a particularly close one – this is the monarch who was the founder of what we know as the Hittite kingdom.

Plate 2

CHAPTER II
Who were the Hittites ?

In 1902 the Norwegian scholar J. A. Knudtzon announced to a sceptical world that he had discovered a new Indo-European language. It was to be found, he claimed, written in a cuneiform script on two clay tablets which had been discovered fifteen years earlier at El Amarna in Egypt among the diplomatic correspondence of the pharaohs Akhenaten (1379–1362) and his father Amenophis III (1417–1379). Since one of the tablets was addressed to the king of a hitherto unknown country called Arzawa, the language was christened Arzawan. Knudtzon's suggestion of an Indo-European connection, though plausible, found little favour with his contemporaries, but it was known that a few fragments of tablets written in the same language had been found at Boğazköy in central Anatolia, and excavations begun there in 1906 soon brought to light an archive of thousands of tablets, many of which were written in 'Arzawan'. There was now ample material for a full linguistic study, the result of which, as announced by B. Hrozný in 1915, was a full confirmation of Knudtzon's claim. The language of the texts was indeed basically Indo-European, and so gave scholars their earliest surviving evidence for a member of that linguistic family.

Important as this discovery was for the philologists, for the historians it brought many problems. Central Anatolia was scarcely the place where they had expected to find early speakers of Indo-European, and they had to ask themselves firstly who these people were, and in the second place how and when they had got there. Fortunately, the first question was easily answered. The tablets themselves showed quite clearly that Boğazköy was ancient Hattusas, the capital of the land of Hatti and the seat of rulers who had, during the fourteenth and thirteenth centuries BC, been among the most important of the Middle Eastern world. Obviously the language of the tablets was that of the kings of Hatti. It was consequently re-christened 'Hittite', and the name 'Arzawan' was quietly forgotten.

Fig. 11 Inscription in 'Hieroglyphic Hittite' from Hamath (after Messerschmidt)

But the solution to this problem raised other problems which demanded answers. It had in fact been suspected for some time that Boğazköy was the capital of the Hittites, but the grounds for this identification seemed to be contradicted by the new evidence. In 1876 A. H. Sayce had suggested that certain basalt blocks inscribed with a hieroglyphic script and found at Aleppo and Hamath in northern Syria were in fact the work of the Hittites, a people hitherto known only from references in the Bible and in the records of Egypt and Assyria. In 1880 Sayce further suggested that a number of rock carvings in southeast, central and western Asia Minor, some of which were associated with the same script as appeared in the Syrian blocks, were also of Hittite workmanship. By 1900 almost a hundred 'Hittite' inscribed monuments of this sort had been recorded. Among these was one which stood in a prominent position among the ruins of Boğazköy, and the natural conclusion was that the site was that of a large and important Hittite city. Consequently it was rather a shock to discover that Hittite records were written in a cuneiform script, for if 'Arzawan' was really Hittite, who wrote in the hieroglyphic script? The issue was complicated by the fact that although the basic decipherment of the cuneiform texts proved to be fairly simple, the hieroglyphic texts were a much more difficult matter. Still, patient work by several scholars succeeded in resolving a large number of their problems, and the discovery of a long bilingual inscription in 1947 provided confirmation for much of their

Fig. 11

Plates 3, 4

work and a great increase in the understanding of the script and language. 'Hieroglyphic Hittite' is also an Indo-European language. Most
of the known texts can now be seen to date from a period after the fall of
the Hittite kingdom, and are the work of south-east Anatolian and
north Syrian monarchs who preserved the name and tradition of the old
Hittite realm; but some texts go back to the hey-day of the Hittite
Empire and are the work of known Hittite monarchs. Yet the language
of these inscriptions, while fairly closely related to that of the cuneiform
texts, is by no means identical with it. Clearly both languages existed
side by side in the Hittite realms, with 'Hieroglyphic Hittite' gradually
playing a larger part. It has been suggested that later Hittite monarchs
were 'Hieroglyphic Hittites' who took over the kingdom of the 'cuneiform' Hittites, and it has even been maintained that latterly cuneiform
Hittite was a dead language used only through the conservatism of royal
scribes. However this may be (and there may well be some truth in it) it
seems clear that the hieroglyphic script and language were introduced
to the Hittite realms from some outside source at a period preceding the
greatest days of the Hittite Empire, perhaps during the second half of
the fifteenth century BC.

What was that outside source? 'Hittite Hieroglyphs' were already in
use in Cilicia by about 1500 BC, as can be seen from the seal of a king
of that area excavated at Tarsus. Another seal found at Beycesultan in
south-western Anatolia and securely dated to the twentieth century BC
bears signs which have been identified by some scholars as 'Hittite
Hieroglyphs'. It has therefore been suggested that the home of this
script, and of the people who spoke the language written in it, was the
southern and south-western part of Asia Minor. The further identification of these peoples is unexpectedly aided by material from the archives
of Boğazköy. As well as cuneiform Hittite, several other languages are
used in these texts, and one of them is named as Luwian. The curious
thing is that 'Hieroglyphic Hittite' is much more closely related to
Luwian than it is to cuneiform Hittite, and the two seem in fact to be
dialect variants of the same language. But we can go further than this.
Luwian is presumably the language of the area known in the cuneiform
texts as Luwiya, and Luwiya can be seen to be the earlier name of an
area referred to in the Hittite Imperial period as Arzawa. And so we
reach the final position that the language originally known as Arzawan

is in fact the language of the Hittites, while the language written in 'Hittite Hieroglyphs' is a dialect of the language of Arzawa.

What and where is Arzawa? A study of the Hittite archives serves to show that the group of states known to the Hittites by this name formed the principal power of western Anatolia, with their centre either in the Turkish 'Lake District', or, more probably, in what was later known as Lydia. The part that they had to play in Hittite history will be detailed in a later chapter. Here it is sufficient to say that it is increasingly clear that Arzawa was a powerful state with considerable influence in both Anatolian and international politics, and that if her records were to be recovered they would tell us a great deal that we would like to know about both the Near Eastern and the Aegean worlds.

To return now to our original argument, it can be seen that between 1400 and 1200 BC large parts of Anatolia were controlled by speakers of Indo-European languages. The north-central area, centred on Hattusas, was the homeland of the Hittites, while the areas south and west of this were occupied by speakers of Luwian and the closely related dialect known as 'Hieroglyphic Hittite', but perhaps better referred to by some neutral term such as 'Anatolian Hieroglyphic'. The history of these peoples has been reconstructed with a fair degree of detail from their surviving records, and so the first question raised above – the identity of those who wrote the texts – can be given a reasonably full answer.

But the second question remains to be answered. The evidence for the original 'homeland' of the Indo-European languages seems to be over-whelmingly against a situation in Anatolia, and this means that speakers of an Indo-European language must have entered Anatolia at some time and from some other area. But from what area? And at what time? On the first point there is now fairly general agreement that the linguistic evidence points to an Indo-European 'homeland' somewhere in the area that stretches from the lower Danube along the north shore of the Black Sea to the northern foot-hills of the Caucasus. In that area it can plausibly be connected with the *Kurgan* or Pit-grave culture whose bearers spread originally from the Eurasian steppes north and west of the Sea of Aral, reached the Black Sea towards the end of the fourth millennium, and during the third millenium penetrated much of Europe from the Baltic to the Aegean. The culture is typified by tumuli (*kurgans*) covering burials in house-type graves, often richly endowed with funeral gifts. If this is accepted, it seems certain that speakers of an Indo-European language must have reached Anatolia from the north, and the only question to be settled is whether they came from the north-west, via the Dardanelles and the Bosporus, or from the north-east, via the passes of the Caucasus. On this issue scholarly opinion has been fairly evenly divided, and it is necessary to turn from linguistic to archaeological evidence. The theory that linguistic changes are necessarily reflected in the archaeological record has recently been strongly attacked,[6] but it is difficult to believe that a new language can be successfully introduced to an area without material change of any kind. At any rate the hypothesis of 'no linguistic change without archaeological change' is one that in the absence of linguistic evidence we are forced to adopt if we are not to abandon hope of solving the problem. Extreme caution is of course required, and if the hypothesis is seen to be contradicted at any point by the linguistic evidence which is available, it must be abandoned at once. But if the linguistic and archaeological evidence are seen to complement one another there is a reasonable chance that the hypothesis may lead towards the truth.

In examining the archaeological evidence from Anatolia it is perhaps best to start in the south-west, where we have seen reason to suppose that there were Indo-European-speakers between 1400 and 1200 B C, with a possibility that they were already there by 2000 B C. Certainly between these two dates there is no sign of an archaeological break at Beycesultan, the principal excavated site for this area, and this helps to confirm the scanty linguistic evidence from the site. But a little earlier than this, at the end of the period known as Beycesultan XIII, there are considerable signs of destruction, and the following level, Beycesultan XII, shows clear signs of change. The new culture, which continued without interruption until the end of the Bronze Age, can be seen to be related in its origins to the culture of the second city of Troy, in north-west Anatolia. This Trojan culture has also many links with the Cilician culture known as EB III. The two have recently been claimed as contemporary,[7] but it seems more probable that there is in fact an overlap between them. Cilician EB III has sufficient connection with cultures further east and south to establish a fairly accurate date for it, and it seems to have lasted from about 2400 to 2000 B C. This gives us a date of perhaps 2200 B C for the end of Troy II and, since there are elements of Troy II, III and IV in Beycesultan XII–VIII, *c.* 2300 BC is a reasonable date for the introduction of the north-western culture to the south-west. If then we may claim that this culture was brought by speakers of an Indo-European language, then this language must have been spoken in north-west Anatolia during the Troy II period, and have reached there from south-eastern Europe at some time early in or before that period. But although both Troy IIa and Troy I were destroyed (*c.* 2500 and *c.* 2600 BC), there is no sign at either time of any intrusive cultural element from Europe. There is a similar lack of new elements at the beginning of Troy I (*c.* 2900 BC?) and even during the preceding Kumtepe Ib period, which takes us back to at least 3000 BC. It has to be admitted, in fact, that the trail cannot at present be followed into south-eastern Europe, and that there are few obvious signs of any *Kurgan* penetration into north-western Anatolia. But one can perhaps see in a carved stone block found in secondary use in a middle Troy I context and bearing a strong resemblance to funeral stelae of a type which often marked *Kurgan* burials, an indication that such a movement was already by that time a thing of the past.

Once arrived in Anatolia, the newcomers' progress can be roughly traced. At first they were content to build up the prosperity of the north-west along local lines, but by about 2600 BC they had reached as far inland as Beycesultan, sacking level XVIIa and introducing a culture of Troy I type. The destruction of Troy Ij, followed by that of Troy IIa, proved only a temporary set-back, and shortly after 2500 the Trojans were sufficiently secure and prosperous to take up trading with distant lands. Contact with Cilicia, presumably by sea, can be seen in the introduction of the potter's wheel to the north-west during phase IIb, and, if the evidence of the Dorak tombs is accepted, communication with Egypt was by this time common enough for the exchange of diplomatic gifts. About 2400 BC the attraction of Cilicia proved so strong that it was largely 'taken over' by north-west Anatolians (not just 'Trojans': the cultures are by no means identical), and Cilicia proved so much more convenient as a trading-centre that the north-west, as represented by Troy II d–g, began to lose its importance. Meanwhile Cilicia continued to prosper, and Cilician influence spread up through the Taurus passes and on to the southern and south-western parts of the plateau, where it can be seen in pottery shapes at Beycesultan (level

Fig. 8

Fig. 12

XIII). But the people of Troy II, their overseas expansion thwarted, began to expand inland once more, and by 2300 BC they had reached and destroyed Beycesultan, and pushed on across the Konya Plain to the foot-hills of the Taurus. The over-all result of these conquests, however, was disastrous. Troy itself could not take advantage of them, for *c.* 2200 it was itself destroyed by fire, without apparently the involve-ment of any outside enemy. In the rest of western and southern Anatolia the over-all impression is that of a grave decline in material culture. While some areas recovered within two or three hundred years, others, like Lycia and Pisidia, seem to have had little settled occupation until the first millenium.

The invasion seems to have spent its strength before it reached Cilicia. In this area there is no change of culture until about 2000 BC, when an intrusive style of painted pottery, often linked with the arrival of the Hurrians, makes its appearance from northern Syria. But an unexpected echo of the Indo-European incursions is perhaps to be found in the legends of the Mesopotamian Dynasty of Akkad.[8] Sargon, the principal monarch of this dynasty, is said in an admittedly late text to have made an expedition about 2300 BC in support of a colony of Mesopotamian merchants settled at Purushanda, and another text, also of later date, refers to the invasion of the Akkadian empire and the destruction of Purushanda by barbarous hordes about 2230 BC. Purushanda is almost certainly to be equated with the Purushattum which is mentioned in later texts from Anatolia, and is most probably situated south of the Salt Lake or in the Konya Plain. If then the legends have any historical value, they imply Akkadian influence through Cilicia and up on to the Konya Plain. If this is so, we can perhaps see the spread of Cilician influence in the same direction between 2400 and 2300, as mentioned above, taking place in conjunction with the spread of Akkadian merchant-colonies. The barbarous hordes of the later attacks could then be identified with the spread of Indo-European-speakers from the north-west reaching the Konya Plain by about 2230.

The foregoing scheme may perhaps account for the 'Luwianizing' of Anatolia south and west of a line drawn from the Bosporus to the Gulf of Iskenderun. In central Anatolia the situation is more complicated. In this area records in an Indo-European language go back to the earliest days of what we know as the Hittite Old Kingdom, about

1650 BC. Only the 'Anittas-text', which deals with the deeds of the kings of Kussara, refers to events earlier than this, and it may in fact be an Old Kingdom translation into Hittite. Even if it was originally written in Hittite at a time contemporary with the events it describes, this takes us back only to about 1780 BC. The period immediately preceding this, from about 1940 to 1780, is amply documented from the records of the Assyrian merchant-colonists. These records frequently contain names of native Anatolians, and for many years an intensive study has been made of these names with a view to tracing the languages spoken at the time. At first scholarly opinion was inclined to the view that only a few names with an Indo-European etymology were to be found, and that not one of these was unmistakably Hittite. This led to the suggestion that at the period known as Karum II (*c.* 1940–1840), to which most of the documents belong, the Hittites had not yet reached central Anatolia, and that the destruction of Karum II about 1840 was in fact an indica-tion of their arrival.[9] A line of destruction was traced from the Caucasus to central Anatolia at about the same time, and this was equated with the route taken by the Hittites from the south-Russian steppes. Against this reconstruction there are several objections. First, and most import-ant, further study of the proper names in the Assyrian documents has shown that Indo-European names are much more numerous than was at first supposed, and that many, including a majority of the local rulers' names, can be regarded as 'proto-Hittite'. Second, many archaeo-logists deny any fundamental break in the archaeological record in Georgia and other areas through which the alleged Hittite invasions must have passed; and third, the linguistic relationship between Hittite and Luwian seems to be too close for one to suppose that they entered Anatolia by such diverse routes. The destruction of Karum II cannot then be accepted as a sign of the arrival of the Hittites. On the contrary, they seem by that time to be already established in a powerful position, and the linguistic evidence can now be seen to agree with what the archaeologists have long been stressing, that central Anatolia in the colony-period is basically Hittite.

What is required then is evidence for a spread of influence to central Anatolia from the areas to the south and west at a period subsequent to the 'Luwianizing' of these areas, but before the colony-period. Archaeo-logically this spread is easy to observe. Hand-made 'depas' (see also

Fig. 12 'Depas' cups. Left to right: Tarsus EB III, Kültepe EB III, Troy II, Beycesultan XIIIa. Not to scale (after Mellaart)

Fig. 12

p. 136) cups at Alişar and Kültepe correspond to those of the so-called 'Trojan' phase in Cilicia; at Kültepe there are also wheel-made plates with the same connection, and grey bottles and other Syrian imports which are likewise common in Cilicia at this time. Other signs may also be observed. The beak-spouted jug, a typically Hittite shape of vessel, is rare in central Anatolia before this period, and it may be suspected that it now appears through the influence of the contemporary culture of south-west Anatolia and Cilicia. Most significant of all is the plan of a large public building at Kültepe. This is in the form of a 'megaron' or *Fig. 13* hall-and-porch, a type of building which is foreign to central Anatolia but which has a long ancestry in the west. Whether it is to be identified as a temple or a palace, it serves to show that people with western connections had achieved positions of considerable power in the area. The dating of these influences can be roughly linked to the Cilician sequence, and the over-all impression is that this period in central Anatolian prehistory begins about 2350–2300 BC.

One important change in the central Anatolian ceramic repertory has not so far been mentioned. This is the sudden appearance of painted 'Cappadocian' pottery which gives a rather exotic touch to the pre-dominantly plain tradition of the area. This painted pottery has often been regarded as a Hittite introduction, but it now seems clear that it was a local development from the simpler painted wares of the immediately preceding period. But the spread of Indo-European influence into central Anatolia can perhaps be seen in the fact that early 'Cappadocian' vessels have painted patterns which repeat the incised ornamentation of pottery found at Beycesultan in levels immediately succeeding the 'Luwian' invasion. Thus although the pottery itself is not a Hittite innovation, some features of its development may be linked with the arrival of speakers of an Indo-European language.

One item of linguistic information may also be added. It has been pointed out that the clearly Hittite words išhiul and išpant- occur in the records of the Assyrian merchants in connection with the place-names Lawazantiya, Nenassa and Ullamma. This suggests that Hittite was spoken in and around these places at a period contemporary with that of the merchant-colonies, and since all three are probably to be located south or south-west of Kültepe we have yet another indication of the direction from which the Indo-Europeanizing movement must have come.

What seems to emerge from all this is a largely peaceful spread of influence – and language – into central Anatolia from the south, and to a lesser extent from the west, shortly after these areas had themselves

Fig. 13 Building of megaron type from Kültepe, c. 2250 BC (after Lloyd)

been 'Indo-Europeanized' from the north-west. The Külteppe megaron shows that the new arrivals had already gained considerable influence there by about 2250, and by the period of the Assyrian merchant-colonies they formed a large proportion of the population, and were clearly even then largely absorbed into the native element. This is only to be expected from the linguistic evidence of the later Hittite texts, where an Indo-European structure is combined with a very large indigenous vocabulary, and from the organization of the Hittite state, which shows no sign of a class-system based on language differences. All this presupposes a long period of previous development with speakers of both Indo-European and non-Indo-European languages present in the population.

At the time of their arrival, the newcomers probably spoke a form of Indo-European that had yet to be differentiated into Hittite, Luwian and other dialects which we know from the later second millennium. For several hundred years Kanesh played the leading part in central Anatolian affairs, but shortly after 1800 the kings of Kussara, a town in the eastern periphery of the area, began to extend their influence west-wards. Kanesh and other central towns were conquered, and eventually Kussara was able to take over the dominant position. A hundred years later, as we have seen in Chapter I, rulers in some way connected with Kussara set up their capital at Hattusas, and by this time their language is recognizably a slightly archaic form of Hittite. The script in which they wrote it is not the same as that of the earlier Assyrian colonists, and was presumably adopted by them from some area, as yet unidentified, to the south-east of Anatolia.

The picture that has emerged from the foregoing discussion is a fairly simple one, but it must be said at once that there are complications. The first of these is the fact that there are other signs of western influence on central Anatolia at a slightly later period than the one described above. About 2000 BC a wheel-made monochrome ware makes its appearance at Kanesh and other central Anatolian sites, and the ancestry of this pottery seems on the evidence of surface surveys to lie in north-west Anatolia, and particularly in the Tavsanli-Kütahya region. The interest-ing point about it is that it is to be found in the earliest levels of occupa-tion at Boğazköy, a fact which suggests that the original settlement at this site was made by north-westerners who were presumably Indo-

European, but not Hittite, in speech.[10] This drive from the north-west may have been the occasion of the establishment of Palaic, another Indo-European dialect known from the Boğazköy records, in the vicinity of Kastamonu, the area in which it was probably spoken in the second half of the second millennium. No linguistic features in the Hittite texts from the Boğazköy archives can yet be ascribed to this wave of western influence. It has in fact been claimed that the movement shows the arrival of the Hittites themselves in central Anatolia, but on the whole it seems to be too late and from the wrong direction to satisfy all the evidence.

Another problem which should be mentioned here is that of the predecessors of the Hittites in central Anatolia. The Boğazköy archives contain texts which are described as being in 'Hattic', a language of a completely different structure from Indo-European, and it is usually supposed that the speakers of Hattic were the inhabitants of the land of Hatti before the arrival of the Indo-European-speaking immigrants. If so, they are presumably to be equated with the people of the EB II or 'copper-age' period which immediately preceded the influences described above. This period is well-known from Kültepe, Alişar and Alaca, and its most spectacular surviving remains are the 'royal' tombs at Alaca, with their famous 'standards' and other metalwork. But although the ordinary people of the royal tomb period may have spoken Hattic, it is by no means certain that the monarchs who occupied the tombs did so as well. Other slightly later tombs with similar metalwork have been discovered at sites which are closer to the Black Sea coast than Alaca, and it has been suggested that the Alaca tombs show the temporary extension of a northern culture into central Anatolia. Apart from the tombs, this northern culture is not well known, but its metalwork is in many ways clearly related to that found at Maikop and *Figs. 6, 7* Tsarskaja in the basin of the Kuban, north of the Caucasus. This Russian culture has reasonably been ascribed to *Kurgan* peoples who had recently come under the influence of higher cultures south of the Caucasus. If so, the occupants of the Alaca tombs, which show many *Kurgan* features, may well also have been *Kurgan* people, speaking an Indo-European language. But there is no sign of any spread of this *Kurgan* culture further south into Anatolia, and so it cannot be linked with the spread of Hittite, to say nothing of Palaic and Luwian. The language of the rulers who were buried in the Alaca tombs, although probably Indo-European, was almost certainly not proto-Hittite.

All of this, of course, brings us no nearer to identifying the Hattians. They *may* have been the peoples of central Anatolia who were temporarily subject to the kings buried at Alaca, and whose remains can also be seen at Alişar and Kültepe, but it has recently been suggested that they *followed* the Hittites from south-east Europe into Anatolia rather than preceding them in the central area.[11] It is also worth mentioning that in the records of the Assyrian merchant-colonies the 'Land of Hatti', whose native language one must assume was originally Hattic, may not have been centred in Hattus/Boğazköy, but have been a good deal further to the east, in the area around modern Divriği. The question 'who were the Hattians?' must at present be left open.

No discussion of the languages of Anatolia can be complete without some mention of the vexed question of Greek-speaking peoples in Anatolia and Luwian-speakers in Greece. It has long been commonly accepted that the Greek language was introduced to Greece by newcomers who brought with them the type of pottery known as 'Minyan'

Fig. 14

ware. For many years the evidence available suggested that this pottery appeared in Greece about 1900 BC, at the beginning of the Middle Helladic period. Since very similar pottery was found at Troy, where it was introduced at approximately the same date (early Troy VI), it seemed an obvious conclusion that there had been a two-pronged

Fig. 14 Greek and Anatolian 'Minyan' ware: l. from Korakou, Middle Helladic period; r. from Tavşanli, Troy V period (after Mellaart)

invasion from somewhere further north, with one group moving down into Greece and the other occupying north-west Anatolia. The inhabitants of Troy VI then spoke an early form of Greek. A further complication was added when it was suggested that Trojan Minyan ware had its ancestry in the latter part of the Early Bronze Age in the region south and east of the Sea of Marmara. The conclusion to be drawn from this was that Greek-speakers had entered north-west Anatolia at some time during the Early Bronze Age, had stayed there for some time, and had then crossed by sea to central Greece at the beginning of the following period, leaving some of their number to develop the culture of Troy VI.[12] More recent research, however, seems to indicate that both these theories are based on false premises. Minyan pottery has been found in Greece in EH III contexts, and, more important, its origins can now be seen to lie not in north-west Anatolia but in the Baden culture centred on Austria-Hungary, a culture which can be linked with the spread of *Kurgan* features into central Europe.[13] Further analysis of Anatolian 'Minyan' suggests that the resemblances between it and Greek Minyan are largely illusory, and that the two have different origins and different developments.[14] So theories that there were Greeks in north-west Anatolia during the Middle and Late Bronze Ages seem to be without foundation. Yet a certain amount of doubt remains. When the north-west emerges into written history in the first millenium it is part of the Greek world, occupied by Greek-speaking peoples. But the arrival of these 'Aeolic' Greeks from Greece, unlike that of the Ionians further south, cannot yet be recognized without doubt in the archaeological record. Only further excavation and research can show whether they were in fact first-millennium immigrants from across the Aegean or the descendants of Greek-speaking natives of the second millennium.

The problem of Luwian-speakers in Greece centres on the many place-names ending in -anthos, -assos and similar forms which are to be found on either side of the Aegean. These endings can be plausibly explained as Luwian, and their distribution suggests that Luwian, or rather its linguistic ancestor, was at some time spoken over large areas of both western Anatolia and Greece. It has been suggested that it was 'Luwians' (rather than Greeks) who arrived in Greece at the beginning of the Middle Helladic period (*c.* 1900 BC), or even that they arrived as late as the Shaft Grave Period (*c.* 1600 BC). But, as was pointed out long ago, there is a remarkable coincidence between the distribution of place-names of this type and that of sites with Early Helladic II connections.[15] The origins of many features of the Aegean Early Bronze Age can plausibly be sought in western Anatolia, and since, accepting the arguments presented above, that area was already by that time proto-Luwian in speech, there is much to be said for a contemporary linguistic spread to the Greek mainland. On this hypothesis Greek was not the first Indo-European language in Greece, but was preceded in the area by a 'proto-Luwian' linguistic element which was widespread during the earlier part of the Early Bronze Age.

CHAPTER III

The Hittites and their Neighbours

In chapter I we saw how trade between Anatolia and Assyria was ended when the routes along which merchandise travelled were cut by the increasingly active Hurrian states of northern Mesopotamia. We saw too how the kings of Kussara took advantage of this situation to gain control of much of central Anatolia. In fact the removal of their capital westward to Kanesh/Nesa was probably a direct result of Hurrian pressure, for Kussara itself was uncomfortably close to the newly emergent powers. Central Anatolia however provided its own problems, for there too there were unruly neighbours, and it was perhaps the presence of such neighbours on the northern frontier of the new realm that led a prince of the royal house about 1650 BC to decide that strategic considerations were of greater importance than the curse of Anittas, and to build a new fortress at the long deserted but naturally defensible site of Hattusas. The Hurrian advance continued, and it may be supposed that when the eastern parts of the realm fell to them Hattusilis – 'man of Hattusas', as the prince now styled himself – found that he was left as an independent monarch with ample opportunity to increase his power. The direction of his expansion was dictated by economic considerations, for the loss of the Assyrian connection had meant also the loss of essential tin supplies, and an alternative route had to be found. The obvious alternative was, as we have seen, the route which ran up the Euphrates valley from Babylonia to the Mediterranean coastlands, and it was towards the control of this route that the policy of the early Hittite monarchs was directed. The rough outlines of this policy can be reconstructed from surviving contemporary documents and later references, complicated as these are by the fact that Hittite historians in examining their own records deduced that the royal title 'Labarnas' referred to a monarch who preceded Hattusilis, whereas it can now be reasonably assumed that events attributed to the time of 'Labarnas' in fact took place during the reign of Hattusilis himself.

Fig. 15

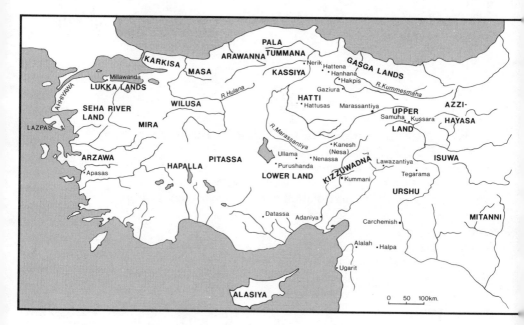

Fig. 15 Map of Anatolia in Hittite times

Fig. 16

The Hittite king's first action was the conquest of the cities that lay between his capital and the Cilician Gates. Once these cities were secured, he could move down into Cilicia and reach the Mediterranean Sea. Here, on the threshold of the Syro-Mesopotamian world, he could build fortresses like that at Mersin (originally ascribed by the excavators to a later period) and make preparation for his attack on the trade-route. The enemy against whom his efforts were directed was Aleppo, the power in command of the northern terminus of the route. But Aleppo was much too strong to be dealt with at one blow. First the Hittite king turned on Alalah, the principal port of the area, thus robbing Aleppo of its outlet to the sea. Fortunately for us, the site of Alalah has been excavated, and the Hittite attack may be convincingly equated

with the destruction of level VII of the site, an event which can be dated
to between 1650 and 1630 B C.[16]

After capturing Alalah, Hattusilis moved north against Urshu and
other allies of Aleppo: but before he could complete the isolation of his
enemy, he turned in a completely different direction. His opponent on
this occasion was Arzawa, which we have already met as the principal
power of western Anatolia. Unfortunately, written documents have
yet to be recovered from this area, and what is known of it comes from
archaeological results and from references in the texts of other peoples,
notably the Hittites and the Egyptians. Even the location of the various
western states is a matter of vigorous dispute, some scholars placing
Arzawa to the south-west of the Hittite homeland, in the Turkish
'Lake District', while others, with a greater degree of probability, locate
it to the west, with its centre in what was later known as Lydia and its

N

0   15
          m

*Fig. 16 Plan of part of town
wall, Mersin. Old Hittite
period (after Garstang)*

capital on the sea-coast somewhere near Smyrna or Ephesus. Indeed the whole picture of western Anatolian geography in the second millennium BC has recently been changing a good deal, and it might be as well to digress at this point and give details of what the picture is. Arzawa is the focal point of the area, and round it are grouped the 'Arzawa countries', closely attached to Arzawa itself by linguistic and dynastic ties. These are Mira, east of Arzawa, Hapalla to the south-east, and the Seha River Land to the north. Wilusa too was sometimes recognized as an Arzawa-country; it lay most probably in or near the rich Eskişehir plain, although many scholars would equate its name with (W)ilion and make it include the site of Troy. Other western countries have given rise to even more discussion. The Lukka Lands are often equated with Lycia, but their connections seem to be with the north-west. They probably lay along the south shore of the Sea of Marmara. Karkisa and Masa too are not to be sited in later Caria and Mysia, but placed east of the Lukka Lands, around and beyond the Gulf of Izmit.

This leaves Millawanda and Ahhiyawa, and brings us to the most controversial question of all. Ever since Forrer's proposal in 1924 that the Ahhiyawans of the Hittite texts were to be equated with the Homeric Achaeans, and consequently with the Mycenaean Greeks, academic opinion has been sharply divided between support and rejection of his view. Philhellenic scholars claim that Hittites and Mycenaeans cannot fail to have made contact in the Aegean and eastern Mediterranean, that the contact, when it is made, is at just the times and at just the places where one might expect it, and that the resemblance of names between the Achaeans and the Ahhiyawans is more than fortuitous. Anti-Mycenaeans allege that archaeologically there is little evidence for contact, that there is nothing in the texts to suggest that Ahhiyawa is outside Anatolia, and that the equation of the names is a philological impossibility. In a conflict of this nature one has to take sides, and the author must admit at once that he is an anti-Mycenaean. This view is based mainly on the wider question of Anatolian geography, for Ahhiyawa and Millawanda, a coastal city under Ahhiyawan influence, are closely connected with states such as the Lukka Lands and the Seha River Land which are (in the author's opinion) to be located in the north-western corner of Anatolia. The Mycenaean theory is largely based on the equation of Millawanda with Miletus, where there is a known

Mycenaean settlement. Attractive though this equation is, it leads to considerable difficulty in arranging the other states of western Anatolia, and must on that account be abandoned. It has to be pointed out, however, that the opposite point of view has very strong academic support, and has recently been persuasively maintained by Professor D. L. Page and others. The historical reconstruction which follows is based on the assumption that Ahhiyawa is in north-west Anatolia and very probably includes territory on the European shores of the Sea of Marmara as well. Those who disagree can follow their own geographical pattern and reinterpret the narrative accordingly, but the author feels a certain amount of justification in claiming that if the arrangement of states suggested above is accepted, the over-all picture of Anatolian geography and history makes sense. Events fit into a general pattern of economic necessity, and the efforts of the various states can be seen to be directed towards something more permanent than the arbitrary ambitions of individual sovereigns.

Perhaps we may now return to Hattusilis and his campaign against Arzawa. Its purpose is unknown. He may have been attacked from behind when his attention was directed to the south-east, but equally his expedition may be linked with one ascribed to 'Labarnas' in a later treaty in the course of which Arzawa and Wilusa were conquered. If we now ask what the importance of Wilusa was, a glance at the map will show us, for Wilusa lay directly across another ancient trade-route – that from the Land of Hatti to north-western Anatolia and across the straits into Europe. It has recently been suggested[17] that this too was a tin-route leading eventually to the rich mines of Bohemia. Certainly central Europe had trade-connections as far afield as Syria not long after the beginning of the second millennium,[18] and towards the end of that millennium a trail of objects with spiral decoration has been taken to show that the Mycenaeans also used the route. But these decorations could equally well have originated in north-west Anatolia, and there is no trace of pottery or anything else that can be unequivocally ascribed to the Mycenaeans. Western Anatolia is little richer in tin than the central area, and we can perhaps see in Bohemia the ultimate source of the tin that was used by the kings of Arzawa. It is then a reasonable guess that in conquering Arzawa and forging a link with Wilusa that was to last almost unbroken for hundreds of years, Hattusilis had the same motive in mind as when he attacked Alalah and the south-eastern route. In each case the object of his campaign was tin.

A Hurrian counter-attack soon forced Hattusilis to turn eastwards again. The whole of the Land of Hatti, except its capital, fell into their hands, but within a year or two the Hittite king had driven them back through the Taurus passes, and was able to advance to the Euphrates. About this time too the ancient capital of Kussara must have been recaptured, and we also hear of successes on the north-eastern frontier. In this area too metal-supplies may have been the ultimate motive for the king's interest. Despite these successes, however, Hattusilis was unable to defeat his first opponent, Aleppo, and he may have received a mortal wound while trying to do so.

His death left the final conquest of north Syria to Mursilis, his grand-son and successor. It occurred to this monarch that diplomacy might bring success where force had failed, so he applied himself to the problem of disrupting the trade-route to his own advantage. Aleppo at its northern end was still much too strong to succumb to Hittite pressure. Babylon at its southern end was weak, but allied to Aleppo. On the middle Euphrates, however, Mari had now disappeared and the new power in the area was the Kingdom of Hana. This state was not under Amorite rule like Babylon and Aleppo, but had recently come under the influence of the Kassites, a foreign people from the Iranian hills. The obvious course was an alliance with Hana to encircle Aleppo, disrupt her trade and reduce her prosperity, and it is probable that this move was made. We have few details of what happened, but about 1595 Mursilis descended from Anatolia and succeeded in destroying Aleppo.

Thus the south-eastern trade-route came under Hittite control at least as far as the middle Euphrates. Mursilis had gained what he needed, but his allies in Hana were not satisfied, and persuaded him that greater glory was at hand. Thus spurred on, Mursilis swept down the Euphrates and descended on Babylon. The dynasty of Hammurabi was brought to a humiliating end, and the Hittites arrived in force on the inter-national field.

The conquest of Babylon cannot have been more than a rash venture by the Hittite king. Physical control of the entire trade-route was not necessary for his purpose and he soon returned to his homeland, leaving the images of the deities of Babylon, and doubtless a part of its treasure, with his allies at Hana. Continuing Hurrian pressure would have made it difficult to hold on to such distant conquests, and palace rivalries in Hattusas also helped in persuading him to withdraw. Shortly afterwards Mursilis was murdered by his brother-in-law, and with his death the Hittite conquests began to crumble away. Under his successors the Hurrians, now led by a dynasty with Indo-Aryan connections, advanced again through north Syria and into Cilicia, the peoples of the northern hills captured the holy city of Nerik and forced the refortification of Hattusas itself, and Arzawa broke away and regained its independence. By the time of the accession of Telepinus (*c.* 1500) the kingdom was confined once again to central Anatolia. Telepinus however was able to consolidate his position sufficiently to advance once more in the direction of north Syria, win several victories in the Anti-Taurus area, and conclude an alliance with the ruler of Kizzuwadna, a new power which had been established in Cilicia by a Hurrian or Indo-Aryan dynasty.

With Telepinus what is usually known as the Old Kingdom comes to an end. Its achievements had been ephemeral, but the policies of its kings set a pattern which was to be followed in all its essentials by the monarchs of the later and greater Hittite Empire. This is the name normally given to the period between about 1450 and 1200 BC. Its history has recently been complicated by the fact that a number of documents, previously assigned to the reign of Tudhaliyas IV towards the end of the period, can now plausibly be taken to describe events in the reign of a much earlier Tudhaliyas, probably the first king of that name, who reigned at the beginning of the Empire. The obscure period between the Old Kingdom and the Empire, sometimes known as the Middle Kingdom, is one of almost unrelieved Hittite decline. Only a treaty with a king of Kizzuwadna shows a temporary success against the Hurrians, now organized and unified as the north Mesopotamian kingdom of Mitanni and eager to gain control of the Euphrates route. At this time too the attraction of northern Syria, with its rich trade and wealth of natural products, brought another major power on to the scene in the shape of Egypt. In 1471 Tuthmosis III advanced up the Levantine coast and conquered Aleppo.

These new developments were highly unwelcome to the Hittites, but they prudently paid tribute to Egypt and waited for their opportunity. It came when Aleppo rebelled against Egypt on the death of Tuthmosis in 1450, but although this rebellion may have been instigated by the Hittites, Aleppo was sufficiently ungrateful to transfer her allegiance to Mitanni. This was the situation when Tudhaliyas I came to the throne shortly after, and his action was swift and decisive. First the alliance with Kizzuwadna was renewed, and within a year or two of his accession he was able to meet and defeat both Aleppo and Mitanni. The south-eastern trade-route was once again in Hittite hands.

Tudhaliyas then turned to the west, and campaigns followed against Arzawa and the Seha River Land. To the north-west, a number of smaller states on or near the route to Europe had banded together to form a confederation under the general name of Assuwa. As this name does not appear in any later document, it must be assumed that after its defeat Assuwa broke up again into its constituent parts. At this time too Ahhiyawa first appears in the Hittite records as a hostile power whose king Attarsiyas at least twice attacked the Hittite vassal Madduwattas. But despite temporary successes in this direction it is clear that Tudhaliyas failed to achieve lasting control of the north-western route.

To the north of the Hittite realms too there was trouble in the Gasga-lands, and further east the Hurrians were making up for their lack of success in north Syria by wooing the kings of the Armenian mountains. It is probable that Tudhaliyas directed a campaign against the north-eastern country known both as Azzi and as Hayasa, and he certainly had to deal with Isuwa, a land which lay across the Euphrates around modern Elazığ. Little is known of this campaign, but it may be pointed out that on the borders of Isuwa are to be found the most important copper-mines in the Middle East (the modern Ergani Maden). These had been known to the Assyrian merchants centuries earlier, and their presence in the border-area between Hatti and Mitanni must surely be regarded as an important factor in the enmity of these powers.

The reign of Tudhaliyas was followed by another period of disaster. North Syria and Kizzuwadna were rapidly lost, and enemies from all sides – the Gasga-lands to the north, Azzi-Hayasa to the north-east, Isuwa to the east, and several other countries besides – closed in on Hattusas and burnt it to the ground. The Land of Hatti was so weakened by these attacks that the king of Arzawa was able to ignore it while he struck across the southern Anatolian plateau towards the approaches to the Cilician Gates. Clearly he too was interested in the south-eastern trade-route, and had ambitions to succeed the Hittite king as an international figure. This can be seen also in the Arzawa letter from El Amarna (mentioned in chapter II) in which the king sought a marriage-connection with the Egyptian royal house. Nothing tells us his plea was successful, but the fact that he made it shows that he regarded himself as the equal of the other Great Kings of the Middle Eastern world.

The triumph of Arzawa did not last. About 1380 the Hittite throne was seized by an energetic young prince called Suppiluliumas, a man who had already before his accession shown by victories in the north-east, north and north-west that he could deal with his country's enemies. An early attack on Mitanni was a failure, although it may have resulted in the temporary recovery of Isuwa. Later, Isuwa was recaptured on a more permanent basis, and Kizzuwadna and the 'Hurri-land', a powerful north Syrian rival of Mitanni, were linked by treaty to the Land of Hatti. Thus Suppiluliumas was in a much stronger position when he moved again against Mitanni, and he very soon gained possession of the lands west of the Euphrates. Aleppo and other north Syrian states were conquered, and the Hittites were once more firmly established at the head of the Euphrates-route.

Suppiluliumas did not repeat his predecessor's mistake by venturing down river to Babylon. Instead he tactfully gained his objective by contracting a marriage with the Babylonian king's daughter. Then a Mitannian counter-attack towards Isuwa was made the pretext for a strong Hittite campaign which succeeded in capturing the Mitannian capital and destroying its remaining power. Finally an attack was mounted on Carchemish, a powerful state situated at the point where the Euphrates comes nearest to the Mediterranean coast, and with its fall Suppiluliumas was able to organize north Syria on a basis which would ensure continuing Hittite supremacy. Carchemish and Aleppo were made into vassal-states under the rule of two of the king's sons, and further east potential danger from Assyria, which had gained its independence at the fall of Mitanni, was counterbalanced by the creation of a new Mitanni subject to the Hittites and acting as a buffer-state against danger from its former subject. Even Egypt almost became a sphere of Hittite influence when the widow of Tutankhamun wrote to Suppiluliumas asking for one of his sons to be her husband. Unfortunately for the Hittite king his son was murdered on the way to Egypt and the proposed alliance did not take place.

In the west Suppiluliumas did not meet with such great success. He had already defeated the army of Arzawa before he came to the throne, and shortly after his accession he drove it back across the Konya Plain from the approaches to the Cilician Gates to Mira and Hapalla. But it is unlikely that the land of Arzawa itself was conquered, and it remained a constant danger to the south-western parts of the Hittite realms.

To the north-west the situation was rather different. Dependent as he was on supplies of tin to equip his forces in Syria, Suppiluliumas made every effort to keep this trade-route open. The Seha River Land was on the whole an effective buffer against aggression from Arzawa, and Ahhiyawa was now a friendly power, probably bound by treaty to the Hittites. The only danger came towards the end of the Hittite king's reign when Millawanda was persuaded by Arzawa to rebel and seek Ahhiyawan assistance. Mira and the Seha River Land were also involved, and the situation must have been rather ugly. Suppiluliumas however was too deeply involved in north Syria to attend to things himself, and the solution of this problem was left to his son Mursilis.

In the north-east Suppiluliumas succeeded in making an alliance with the king of Azzi-Hayasa, but the northern Gasga-people were a constant source of trouble, and yearly campaigns were necessary to cope with their unending raids.

Suppiluliumas died about 1346 of a plague which his soldiers had brought back from a Syrian campaign. His eldest son quickly followed him to the grave, and the throne passed to his younger son Mursilis, who proved to be an effective successor to his father. Fortunately for him, there was no need for immediate action to defend the south-eastern route. The buffer-state of Mitanni, backed by the armed forces of Carchemish, was able for a time to absorb the aggressive energies of Assyria, and Egypt was still recovering from a period of weakness and was as yet unwilling to extend her influence into north Syria. Thus Mursilis was able to attend to the north-western route. Millawanda, which had caused trouble at the end of his father's reign, was quickly defeated. Then Mursilis mounted a full-scale and highly successful attack on the Arzawa lands. On its conclusion Arzawa itself was awarded to a presumably pro-Hittite member of its royal family, while

Mira, Hapalla and the Seha River Land were created separate vassal-
states, bound by elaborate treaties to the Land of Hatti. Thus Arzawa
was encircled by a line of states which separated her both from the Land
of Hatti and from the tin-route. Clearly Mursilis hoped that he would
have no more trouble in the west, and for the remainder of his lifetime
and throughout that of his successor his policy proved remarkably
effective.

In other directions Mursilis met with similar success. The Gasga-
people continued their attacks from the north, and finally Mursilis
established a firm line of border-fortresses under military control which
did succeed in containing his enemies, if not in conquering them.
Further east Azzi-Hayasa rebelled but was defeated again, and in Syria
Mitanni, which had eventually fallen to the Assyrians, was probably
recaptured. All over the empire the emphasis was on good organization
and firm control through vassal-states, a policy which became increasingly necessary with the revival of Egypt and the renewal of her interest in
northern Syria. The latter part of Mursilis's reign was certainly directed
towards preparation for the inevitable clash of powers, and there is no
record of any further expansionist policy at this time. In the far north-
west there was a certain amount of trouble from Piyamaradus of Millawanda, an unruly vassal who had transferred his allegiance to Ahhiyawa.
Mursilis, preoccupied by the growing danger from Egypt, was content
to lead an expedition to Millawanda and ask for the extradition of
Piyamaradus, who had fled to an area under Ahhiyawan control. His
request was probably granted, and it is likely that Piyamaradus gave a
promise of good conduct and was restored to his throne.

The reign of Muwatallis (*c.* 1306–1294) is rather poorly documented,
as the destruction of Hattusas by the Gasga-people and the growing
danger from Egypt caused him to move his capital from Hattusas to a
more southerly site, perhaps near modern Karaman,[14] and the full
records of his reign have yet to be discovered. The growing menace
from the south also made it even more vitally important that there should
be no trouble in the west. Yet Arzawa was restive, and in the north-west
Piyamaradus was misbehaving again. So a quick western campaign
was necessary, and although no details are known, it was clearly a
success. The loyalty of the vassal-states was assured, the king of Arzawa
was flattered by being given a privileged position among them, and the

Seha River Land, the vital buffer between Arzawa and the tin-route, was bound even more closely to the Hittite realms. The result was that when the Egyptian attack finally came, large contingents from the western states served in the Hittite army. But Hittite control must have been rather precarious, for it can be seen that Muwatallis regarded the west as a source of potential rebellion. Clearly disaffection was liable to break out at any moment.

Along the northern border skirmishing with the Gasga-people continued, but with one disastrous exception the fortified line established by Mursilis held, and this meant that the northerners could be kept in check by a comparatively small number of troops. Thus almost all the forces of the Hittite Empire could be concentrated where they were most needed, in north Syria, to meet the advance of the Egyptian pharaoh Rameses II. When the two armies met, at Qadesh on the River Orontes in 1300, the result was a victory for the Hittites, and their control of northern Syria remained unimpaired.[20] Yet the war had very serious consequences for Muwatallis, for while his efforts were concentrated on stopping Egypt, Assyria took advantage of the situation to defeat Mitanni and make it an Assyrian vassal.

Fig. 45
Plate 5

Thus despite the glorious victory of Qadesh, the Hittite Empire was in considerable danger from both east and west. When Muwatallis died about 1294 the situation rapidly worsened, for throughout his short reign his son Urhi-Teshub, who succeeded as Mursilis III, was preoccupied by a quarrel with his uncle Hattusilis, whom he rightly suspected of having designs on the throne. On this issue the lands of western Anatolia were sharply divided. The Seha River Land was strongly in favour of Hattusilis, while Mira and possibly Ahhiyawa supported Mursilis. The course of events is obscure, but it is clear that after the deposition and exile of Mursilis by Hattusilis (*c.* 1287) most of the western lands disappear from the Hittite records. Hattusilis boasts that all those who were well-disposed to his predecessors were equally well-disposed to him, but there is little or no evidence to substantiate this claim for western Anatolia. One has to assume that the Arzawa-lands took advantage of the situation to shake off Hittite control. Only in the north-west, along the vital tin-route, did the Hittites make any effort to retain an interest. Fighting in the Lukka Lands is mentioned in the fragmentary annals of Hattusilis, and the Seha River Land remained a Hittite dependency. Millawanda may have been a Hittite vassal again, and gifts were still exchanged between Hatti and Ahhiyawa.

The situation in Syria was almost as serious. Egypt had been defeated, but Adadnirari I of Assyria had taken advantage of a revolt in Mitanni to incorporate all the territory as far as the Euphrates into his realm. The south-eastern route was thus in great danger. A hasty and transitory alliance was arranged with Babylon, and finally the mutual danger brought Hattusilis and Rameses together. Their treaty stressed the reality of Hittite control over northern Syria, and the Egyptian renuncia- tion of claims to that area, but clearly the agreement was largely meaning- less. While the Hittite king was engaged in making arrangements for his *Fig. 17* daughter to marry Rameses, or for a summit meeting somewhere in Palestine, the Assyrians were consolidating their position further east and moving up into the hills which bordered on Anatolia. The climax to this movement came after Hattusilis had been succeeded (*c.* 1265) by his son Tudhaliyas IV, and Shalmaneser I had followed Adadnirari

Fig. 17 Hattusilis III brings his daughter to be married to Rameses II. From an Egyptian relief at Abu Simbel (after Pritchard)

on the throne of Assyria. In a campaign which reached the Euphrates near Malatya, Shalmaneser must have succeeded in finally wresting from Hittite hands the control of the copper-mines of Isuwa.

The loss of his richest metal-source was a serious blow to the Hittite king, although it was partially offset by the fact that further south, around Carchemish, Hittite forces had succeeded in containing the Assyrian advance. This meant that the ports of the Syrian coast were still in Hittite hands, and it was probably with the help of a Syrian fleet that Tudhaliyas invaded Cyprus, where he could find ample supplies of copper safe from Assyrian attack. To make this doubly certain, a Hittite treaty with Amurru, on the Syrian coast, included a clause prohibiting commercial relations of any kind between Amurru and Assyria.

Thus along the south-eastern trade-route the position remained temporarily favourable to the Hittites. In the north-west similar pressures were building up. Trouble in the Seha River Land was probably caused by Millawanda and backed by Ahhiyawa, and although Tudhaliyas was successful in gaining a victory, it is clear that his control of the trade-route was slipping. Ahhiyawa was growing stronger, and could now be regarded – though temporarily or mistakenly – as one of the great powers of the Middle Eastern world. Arzawa too must have had an important part to play, but its relations with the other states of Anatolia, and with the Mycenaean Greeks along the Aegean coast, must await future discoveries for their clarification. It is clear, however, that the end of the Hittite Empire was at hand.

The successors of Tudhaliyas could do little to restore the situation. About 1240 Tukulti-Ninurta I of Assyria was able to cross the Euphrates and deport thousands of Hittite subjects. In Syria the vassal-states were becoming lax in fulfilling their obligations, to the north the Gasga-people were an ever-present menace, and to the north-west there is an ominous silence. A temporary revival took place under a second Suppiluliumas who won the support of the Syrian vassals once more, attacked the rebellious island of Cyprus, and even led a campaign into upper Mesopotamia in which he may have regained the Isuwan copper-mines and precipitated the downfall of Tukulti-Ninurta. But all this was in vain. When the final blow came, it was not Assyria which delivered it. Far to the north-west a great migration was beginning

Fig. 18
Plate 6

which was to be stopped only on the borders of Egypt.[21] The reasons for this movement and the identity of the peoples who took part in it have been much discussed without any certain conclusions being reached, but it is evident that by the time the invasions reached Egypt both Aegean and Anatolian peoples were involved in it. Yet whatever elements may have made up the invading force, its effect on Anatolia is clear. The north-western trade-route was the first to be cut. Arzawa, the great rival of the Hittites for its use, could not take advantage of the situation, for she too was swept away as the invaders moved down the Aegean coast and on along the Mediterranean shore. Cilicia fell to them, then Cyprus, and the great copper-source had gone. Finally the invaders reached and ravaged north Syria, causing the Hittites' second life-line to be severed. What happened afterwards at Hattusas is by no means clear. No Aegean seafarers came sailing up the Halys, but the centre of the empire was so weakened by the loss of the trade-routes that it could no longer resist the attacks of the ever-present Gasga-people and their neighbours to the north and east. The land of Hatti was destroyed, and its capital was burnt to the ground.

So the Hittite Empire disappeared and was quickly forgotten. For two hundred and fifty years it had maintained its place as a leading power in the Middle Eastern world by a policy of keeping control of the routes by which vital raw materials reached it. This policy had been devised by the monarchs of the Old Kingdom, and its full implementa-tion during the Imperial period gave the Hittites a position of strength and authority from which no other Middle Eastern state could dislodge them. Only when a completely new element was introduced and the trade-routes were cut by barbarian invasions from the north-west did this policy finally fail, and its failure, as Professor Goetze has said, marked the end of an epoch.

Perhaps this is a suitable point at which to mention several mistaken ideas of the nature of Hittite power. The first of these is that the Hittites owed their dominant position to their monopoly of the production of a secret weapon called iron. For this there is, as far as I know, no evidence at all.[22] Secondly, it has been suggested that the superiority of the Hittites was due to the fact that they were ruled by an Indo-European aristocracy. The myth of Indo-European super-intelligence has been exploded long ago, but it is perhaps worth while to point out again that by the time of the foundation of the Hittite Old Kingdom (*c.* 1650) the invasion by speakers of an Indo-European language was already an event of the distant past, and that there is little or no evidence to suggest that the class-structure of the Hittite realm was based on considerations either of language or of race. The Hittites, like other peoples before and after them, were thoroughly hybrid in their racial make-up. Finally, the Hittites have been pictured as a horde of barbarous mountaineers who in 1595 flooded out from behind their barriers and descended, open-mouthed with greed and wonder, upon the ancient civilizations of Mesopotamia. I hope I have shown that Anatolia before the Hittite descent on Babylon was by no means as barbarous as this theory would have us think. On the contrary its traditions were as ancient, and its standards as high, as those of most parts of the contemporary Middle East. I have also tried to show that Hittite interest in Mesopotamia was based on economic principles which were rather more rational than simple barbarous greed.

The break-up of the political units known to us as the Hittite Empire and Arzawa did not of course mean the complete elimination of all those who spoke the Indo-European languages of Anatolia. Linguistic and archaeological research-work is gradually dispelling the gloom of the Dark Age which followed the invasion of the 'Sea Peoples', and revealing the movements that took place within Anatolia, and the new political units which were formed. A great deal of work remains to be done, but it seems increasingly clear that we cannot now postulate four hundred years of chaos and an almost complete return to nomadic conditions.

Fig. 18

Fig. 18 An ox-cart loaded with 'Sea People' under attack by the Egyptians. From an Egyptian relief at Medinet Habu (after Yadin)

Anatolia continued to play an important part in the life of the Aegean and the Middle East. Its mineral and agricultural wealth were still an enormous attraction to neighbouring peoples, and the increasing use of iron after about 1200 BC served only to increase that attraction. The primary trade-routes of the preceding era are still the key to an understanding of the period, and while much has still to be learned about the states on and near the north-western route, the history of the struggle for the routes leading to the south-east can be reconstructed with a fair degree of certainty. The states involved in this struggle are for the most part new ones which rose to power in the political vacuum left by the collapse of the Hittite Empire, but in many cases their traditions and their language link them directly with their great predecessor.

The first indication of the new state of affairs is to be found in the records of Assyria. About 1160 BC the Assyrian provinces of Alzi and Puruhuzzi, situated (significantly?) in the area of the Ergani Maden copper-mines, were invaded by a great army of Muski from central Anatolia, and fifty years later an Assyrian counter-attack, led by Tiglath-Pileser I, had to deal not only with Muski but with Gasga as well. Clearly the Gasga had expanded from their northern homeland across central Anatolia since the fall of the Hittite Empire, and their allies the Muski probably came from the same direction. In the central area itself the archaeological evidence suggests a number of small principalities characterized by petty chieftains' castles and by the use of a new painted pottery usually known as 'Phrygian'. This pottery, however, seems to have no connection with the west, and to be confined to central Anatolia until the eighth century. Theories derived from comparisons with Greek Geometric pottery which suggest that there was little or no occupation in central Anatolia until the same period do not seem to be borne out by the archaeological evidence, and may be based on false premises.

Fig. 19

The Assyrian advance towards Anatolia was not confined to the Ergani Maden route. In 1110 Tiglath-Pileser I reached the Malatya region and encountered a kingdom called Milid which he refers to as 'Great Hatti'. Later in his reign he had contact with another king of Great Hatti, probably at Carchemish, and it can be seen that these and other political units claiming to be the successors of the Hittite Empire had by this time reorganized themselves round the old trade-routes and river-crossings. Inscriptions from these states show that their language was a Luwian dialect written in 'Hittite Hieroglyphs', and it may be assumed that their population was a combination of local peoples and Luwian-speaking groups driven from the plateau by the advance of the Gasga and the Muski. Both of these elements had been part of the Hittite Empire long enough to consider themselves its natural heirs.

Strategically placed as they were, the 'Neo-Hittite' states could not expect their control of the trade-routes to go unchallenged. Assyrian encroachments about 1100 have already been mentioned, and soon after this a new danger appeared in the shape of the Aramaeans, nomads from east of the Euphrates who succeeded in seizing several Hittite principalities and establishing themselves in them. The Aramaean incursions had a serious effect on the Assyrians as well as the Hittite states, and it was not until after 900 BC that Assyrian armies again reached northern Syria and began to penetrate the mountains of Anatolia. For a century the north Syrian states were subjected to a constant series of Assyrian campaigns which produced large amounts of tribute but no permanent conquest. On the Anatolian plateau the Muski were still active in the areas overlooking the Syrian plain, but in the background we can begin to see what must have been the principal power of central Anatolia – the land of Tabal. This state, Luwian-speaking and centred probably on the region of modern Kayseri, was to play an increasing part in the struggle for the trade-routes. Its relation to the producers of the painted 'Phrygian' pottery mentioned above is still problematical, but to call this pottery 'Tabalian' is perhaps less likely to be wrong than to use the name 'Phrygian' for it.

The first Assyrian monarch to come into contact with Tabal was Shalmaneser III, who after reducing the more southerly Neo-Hittite states crossed the Amanus in 838 BC and advanced through what had once been called Kizzuwadna and was now known as Que. The cities of Kizzuwadna and Lawazantiya (near modern Sar and Elbistan) fell to him, and two years later he was able to cross the Anti-Taurus, destroy the cities of Tabal, and receive the submission of its kings. The most important of these rulers was called Tuwatis, a monarch whose inscription in hieroglyphs has survived at Topada. After his victory Shalmaneser turned south-west towards Hubusni (modern Ereğli) and returned through the Cilician Gates and across the Amanus again.

One of the less expected results of centuries of Assyrian and Aramaean pressure on the hills to their north was the enforced union of a number of hitherto independent peoples of the Armenian mountains and beyond into a state known as Urartu. By about 800 this new power was sufficiently strong to extend its influence westwards towards Milid, Tabal and other Luwian-speaking states. By 750 even the king of Carchemish was a vassal of Urartu. This brought Urartu face to face with Assyria, and when in 742 the vital battle was fought the Assyrians emerged as victors. From then on Urartu was no longer a serious rival in the struggle for the resources of Anatolia, and without her support the Neo-Hittite states of northern Syria were unable to resist Assyrian pressure and were quickly absorbed.

This brought Assyrian forces once more to the borders of Anatolia, where Tabal, now ruled by Washu-Sharma, was still the dominant state. Allied to Tabal were several smaller kingdoms clustered round the routes through the Taurus–Tuhana (near modern Niğde) whose ruler has left us his portrait and hieroglyphic inscription at Ivriz, Tunna (near Bulgar Maden), Ishtunda (Karatepe on the River Ceyhan) and Hupisna (perhaps at modern Ereğli). Gasga too were still present, though their precise location is unknown. South of the Taurus and Anti-Taurus mountains lay Que, in an area more open to Assyrian attack. At first these states were quick to offer tribute, but their submission was only temporary, for within a few years Tabal was growing restive again and King Urikki of Que (who appears in a hieroglyphic inscription as Awarikus of Adana) was engaging in subversive correspondence with Urartu. Fortunately for Assyria messages sent from Que to Urartu had to pass through the land of the Muski, where they were intercepted by its still loyal king Mita. Little is known of what happened, but no more is heard of Urikki of Que, and about 730 Washu-Sharma of Tabal was deposed and replaced by the pro-Assyrian Hulli, 'son of nobody'.

Even this was not sufficient to ensure the loyalty of the Anatolian kingdoms, for by 717 there was further trouble in Tabal, and a new anti-Assyrian coalition had been formed consisting of Tabal, the formerly loyal Mita of Muski, and even the king of Carchemish. Assyrian reaction was inevitable. Carchemish was captured while Mita was still trying to fight his way through Que, then Mita was driven back and defeated in his own province, and finally Hulli of Tabal was replaced by his son Ambaris, who was diplomatically married to an Assyrian princess and given the province of Hilakku, probably round modern Karaman, as a dowry. Finally in 712 Ambaris too was deposed and Tabal became an Assyrian province.

The fall of the most important kingdom of central Anatolia meant that Mita of Muski, defeated but unconquered, was the only survivor of the original alliance. Any reconstruction of the events of the next few years is full of uncertainties, but it is clear that Mita must have been driven back from the position between the upper Tigris and Euphrates which the Muski had held for four hundred years, and if one can accept the identifications of a number of frontier-forts held by the Muski at this time, it seems that Mita must have retreated north-west until he was within the great bend of the river Halys. Here he might well have remained, safely outside the reach of the Assyrians, had it not been for events beyond his control further north and east. In 714, just as Mita was in retreat before the advancing Assyrians, the Cimmerians, a horde of fierce warriors from southern Russia, broke through the Caucasus and descended on Urartu. From there they turned west along the south shore of the Black Sea, set up a base in the vicinity of Sinope, and moved southwards towards Tabal. The effect of this movement was to compress Mita between two hostile forces, and his only way of escape lay westwards along the old route towards the Aegean coast and the Sea of Marmara. It was by moving along this route that Mita of Muski disappeared from the Assyrian-dominated lands of central Anatolia and emerged on the periphery of the Greek world as Midas of Phrygia.

It need hardly be said that this account of the history of King Midas does not agree with the accounts preserved by Greek folk-memory. According to this the Bryges or Phrygians crossed into Anatolia from south-eastern Europe shortly before the Trojan War, and more modern historians have seen in the presence of Muski about 1150 on the upper Tigris and Euphrates evidence of the furthest penetration of this European people. However no archaeological evidence has been found to support such far-reaching activity, and in fact when evidence becomes more abundant it points much more strongly to a movement from east to west, rather than in the other direction. Certainly there are signs of movements into Anatolia from south-east Europe around 1200 BC. In the north-west the site of Troy (level VIIb2) shows the introduction of crude

hand-made pottery known as Knobbed Ware which seems to have an *Fig. 19*
ultimate affinity with wares of the Late Bronze Age in Hungary and
central Europe. Further east, at the later Phrygian capital of Gordion in
the Sangarius valley, hand-made black pottery appears at about the
same time. The two wares are not directly related, but may have a
similar ultimate origin. At Gordion the new pottery is introduced
without any signs of a break in the continuity of the site, and quickly
disappears as though the newcomers to the site had been absorbed. In
fact Gordion seems, from the limited evidence at present available, to
have developed peacefully and virtually without interruption, and it is
difficult to see in the makers of the black hand-made pottery a conquering
aristocracy who swept across Anatolia to the frontiers of Assyria.

Despite the continuity at Gordion, there are signs of large-scale
movements in western Anatolia between 1200 and 700 BC. Troy
VIIb2 was destroyed about 1100 BC, and in the south-west the site of
Beycesultan (level I) was destroyed about 1000 BC and not reoccupied.
Historical records when they become available again show a pattern of
occupation completely different from what it had been in the Late
Bronze Age, but there is a curious similarity of names which must have
some historical explanation. Lycians, Carians and Mysians may well be
the descendants of the inhabitants of Bronze Age Lukka, Karkisa and
Masa, but they have been forced from their former homes and pushed
down the Aegean coast to the areas where they are to be found in the
Classical period. The pressure behind this movement presumably came
from Europe, but no details of those who exerted it are known. It was
perhaps at this time that groups such as the Mygdones, the tribe of the
Phrygian eponymous hero Mygdon, crossed into Anatolia and settled
in the region of modern Iznik and the lower Sangarius valley, driving
the original inhabitants (the Masa) from their homes and starting a
movement which ended only when the Lukka-people reached Lycia
in the far south-west. In their new homes these peoples continued to use
their Luwian dialects, as can be seen from inscriptions written by them
in the Classical period. In these 'Late Luwian' kingdoms we can in
fact see the last survivors in western Anatolia of the political units of the
second millennium.

Where Phyrgia is concerned, its capital city Gordion remains a
typically western Anatolian town until the late eighth century, when

Fig. 19 'Knobbed Ware' from Troy VIIb;
Phrygian pottery decoration, fibula and
writing

there is a rapid increase of eastern influence in the shape of painted pottery, cauldrons of Urartian type, and fibulae which have connections with south-east Anatolia and northern Syria. Most important of all is perhaps the appearance of alphabetic writing in conjunction with these eastern features at a period which antedates any Greek import to Gordion.[23] It now seems possible that the development of the alphabet from the Phoenician system of writing, and its introduction to Greece, did not take place only through Greek contacts in Levantine ports, as has long been supposed. It may be that the original inspiration towards alphabetic writing took place in south-east Anatolia, where Phoenician and Luwian were written and spoken side by side (as for instance in the Karatepe bilingual), and that when Assyrian pressure forced monarchs such as Mita of Muski towards the north-west they brought with them not only bowls and safety-pins but the new script as well. From Gordion it could have been passed on to the Greek settlements on the Aegean coast (Midas is said to have married a princess of Cyme in Aeolis), and from there to the western world.

The scanty evidence of the Phrygian language which has survived suggests that Phrygian, like the tongues of the other Anatolian states of the time, is basically a member of the Hittite-Luwian group. In following the further history of this group we find that the dominance of Midas of Phrygia did not last long, for shortly after 700 the Cimmerians followed him to his new capital and forced him to commit suicide. At the same time they advanced southwards through Tabal until in 679 they were stopped by the Assyrians just north of the Cilician Gates. For the next fifty years they kept up a constant pressure, with the result that the kingdoms of Tabal and Hilakku were forced into a policy of alternate resistance to Assyria and appeals to her for help. Further west the fall of Gordion had left the leadership of western Anatolia vacant, and the position was now filled by Lydia, a state situated in what had once been the centre of Arzawa. Linguistically Lydian too is related to the Hittite-Luwian group, but the curious thing is that unlike most of its contemporaries it seems to be Hittite rather than Luwian. One has to assume that in the disturbances following the collapse of the Hittite Empire a central Anatolian group had seized power among the ruins of Arzawa, and a memory of this may be preserved in the Herodotean story of a Heraclid dynasty with eastern connections which gained power in Lydia about 1200 BC. One king of this dynasty has the name of Myrsilus, and we may see in him a late descendant and namesake of the Hittite king Mursilis.

By about 660 BC Lydia too was forced to seek Assyrian help against the Cimmerians, and although a temporary respite was gained, it was not until about 630 that the Assyrians were able to defeat the invaders in the south-east, while Lydia was not freed from them until about 610.

With the final defeat of the Cimmerians the native kingdoms of central Anatolia regained their independence, for by this time Assyrian power had been finally broken by events nearer home. The principal beneficiary was Hilakku, while the Lydians were able to advance as far as the Halys in an attempt to fill the gap left by the Assyrian departure. But Anatolia was too important to be left alone for long. In 612 Assyria fell to the Medes and Babylonians, and by 600 the Babylonians were in Cilicia (known to them as Hume), while the Medes were advancing through the Armenian mountains. By 585 the Medes had penetrated as far as the Halys, where they met and fought a drawn battle with the Lydians. At the peace-talks that followed the arbitrators were, according to Herodotus, 'Labynetus of Babylon' and 'Syennesis of Cilicia' – presumably the Babylonian governor of Hume and the king of Hilakku. Again peaceful conditions returned for a few years until in 550 Cyrus of Persia defeated and deposed the king of Media and so created another vacuum in central Anatolia. Croesus of Lydia was quick to cross the Halys in an attempt to gain what he could, and at the same time Cyrus led his army through the mountains to defend the empire he had seized. On this occasion the arbitrators in the 585 agreement took opposite sides, Hilakku favouring Cyrus while Babylon supported Croesus. In 546 Croesus was defeated and the Lydian kingdom was incorporated into the Persian Empire. Hilakku's support of Cyrus was rewarded by the gift of Hume, and it was now for the first time that the name Hilakku/Cilicia was applied to the coastal plain south of the Taurus Mountains. For almost a hundred and fifty years Cilicia was a vassal-kingdom within the Persian Empire until it was fully incorporated and became a province in 401.

The Persian conquest of Anatolia really brings the political history of its Hittite-Luwian-speaking peoples to an end. In central Anatolia the Greeks knew of groups whom they called 'White Syrians', and it may be that this name was given to them because they spoke the same language as the Greeks had found when they first reached Syria – the hieroglyphic Luwian of the Neo-Hittite kingdoms. In western and southern Asia Minor from Caria to Cilicia it can be seen that Hittite-Luwian languages were spoken throughout the Classical period, and traces of them have been found surviving into the Christian era. In the survival of the native language of Isauria, as recorded by patristic writers of the sixth century AD, we can perhaps see the final remnant of a linguistic movement into Anatolia which had taken place more than three thousand years before.

CHAPTER IV
Daily Life in
Late Bronze Age Anatolia

Excavations at second-millennium sites in Anatolia have yielded a fair amount of information on the conditions in which people lived and worked. At Boğazköy, Alaca, Beycesultan and Tarsus sufficiently large areas have been cleared to give a reasonable picture of the layout and domestic architecture of an Anatolian town. It can be seen at once that some attention was paid to over-all town-planning. Streets had a strong tendency to be straight if the lie of the land allowed it, and were often well finished with a surface of coarse gravel. In an area where almost every site was on sloping ground, systems of terracing were constantly necessary, and a great deal of attention had to be given to problems of drainage and water-disposal. Many streets had large drainage-channels, painstakingly built and roofed with stone slabs, running down the middle and connected to lesser channels or clay pipes which carried dirty water into them from the houses on either side. Similar channels drained public buildings and crossed open spaces. The whole system strongly suggests an organized municipal administration.

Within the areas bordered by the streets there is often much less evidence of planning. Houses were of very varied shapes and sizes, and the principal impression can often be one of complete irregularity. Builders in Hittite territory, although they invariably adopted a vaguely rectangular plan, seem not to have believed in accurate right angles or in a regular layout of rooms. Their simple object was to utilize all the space that was available on the site. Sometimes a standard house-pattern can be seen. At Boğazköy, for instance, just outside the temenos-wall of the main temple, there is a group of houses, each consisting of a courtyard with two rooms behind, built back-to-back and opening into parallel lanes. In other cases all that can be said is that there was a principal room or courtyard with a number of lesser rooms joined to it. It should be stressed that the courtyard, if there was one, was not normally placed centrally as a formal feature, but was much more a front yard used for domestic purposes.

Fig. 21

Plate 7

Fig. 20

Plate 8

Fig. 22

Fig. 20 Part of the
drainage-system at Alaca
(after Koşay and Akok)

Fig. 21 Plan of
excavated area, Alaca II
(after Koşay and Akok)

0   50
                      m

Fig. 22 Plan of houses north of Temple I, Boğazköy. A, courtyard; B, lane (after Naumann)

0   30 m

Fig. 23 Houses in Area 'A', Beycesultan Level II. A, courtyard; B, porch-room; C, inner room; D, hearth; E, sink (after Lloyd)

0   5 m

In the south-west, at Beycesultan, a slightly different pattern can be seen. This consisted of a courtyard, off which lay a 'porch-room' with a wide opening supported on wooden posts. Beyond the porch-room were inner rooms whose lay-out differed from house to house. Another house at the same site had the form of a megaron or hall-and-porch, with subsidiary room along one side.

Fig. 23

Fig. 24

63

Fig. 24 The 'Little Palace' area at Beycesultan, Level II (after Lloyd)

Fig. 25

The standard building-material was mud-brick on a foundation of stones, but in areas where stone was freely available it could entirely replace mud-brick, and timber reinforcement often occurred in more wooded areas. Upper storeys were sometimes added, and in some cases a sloping site allowed basement store-rooms to be constructed at one end of a building, with the living-quarters presumably above. Sometimes part of the courtyard was roofed over. Windows, if they existed at all,

64

were small and high up in the walls, and roofs were flat, composed of brushwood and dried mud supported on wooden beams. Interior arrangements were fairly rudimentary. Hearths and ovens were of course a necessity, and stone sinks connected to drains occur, but apart from that there was little in the way of furniture. Paved areas within some houses may have been wash-rooms or toilets, and clay baths in sizes suitable for adults and children, some with built-in seats, have been found. For the rest, people worked, ate and slept at floor level.

The houses of lesser citizens, though normally self-contained units, were usually built together in blocks enclosed by roads or lanes. Free-standing houses also occurred, which must in many cases have been occupied by men of greater wealth or higher position. A house such as that near the Lion Gate at Boğazköy probably belonged to a fairly well-

Fig. 26

Fig. 25 Reconstructions of houses at Alaca (after Koşay and Akok)

Fig. 26 *Plan of a house near the Lion Gate, Boğazköy (after Naumann)*

Fig. 27 *'Castles' at Boğazköy. Left, Sarikale; top right, Nişantepe; bottom right, Yenicekale. C, courtyard; K, 'keep' (after Naumann)*

Fig. 27

to-do private citizen, but other buildings in the upper part of the city were built on outcrops of natural rock and were clearly 'castles' in which members of the ruling class lived. Such buildings were adapted to the positions they occupied, and again it is difficult to see any regular pattern. The building on Nişantepe manages to preserve a fairly rectangular form, and with rooms opening off three sides of a courtyard and probably a staircase to an upper storey, it offers a rather more formal plan than the houses in the lower town. On Sarikale there was a building which fairly closely resembles our idea of a castle – a tower-like 'keep' on the highest and most precipitous part of the rock approached by a tortuous path through an outer system of multiple defensive walls. The castle in Yenicekale is irregular in outline, and little can be said of it except that it consisted of several rooms and was approached through a walled courtyard built on the neck of rock which connected the site to level ground. The reconstruction offered is of an extremely tentative nature.

A good example of the more pretentious type of house has been excavated just inside the main gate at Alaca. The building is constructed on a stone foundation, and the floors are raised above the level of the street outside. The stones of the foundation which show above street level are alternately light and dark in colour, and provide a very rare instance of attention to external decoration in domestic architecture.

Fig. 28

Fig. 28 Plan and reconstruction of house near Sphinx Gate, Alaca (after Koşay and Akok)

The plan of the building is formal, though by no means completely symmetrical, with a recessed central porch on the north side leading to a central court off which the rooms of the house open. From its size and position the house must have been occupied by an important local dignitary.

Elsewhere less can be said about larger houses. At Beycesultan the so-called 'Little Palace' consists of two local courtyard-and-porch-room units joined side by side, with the addition of a sort of ante-room at one end. At Tarsus a two-storeyed building built round three sides of a court seems to have been used as an official residence or for administrative purposes. Apart from an outer court and a large inner room there is little that can be said about its architectural details.

Accommodation inside individual houses may sometimes have been provided for animals as well as humans. At Tarsus, in a large house built on a sloping site, which has been described as a 'governor's residence' on the strength of the number of clay seal-impressions found there, a semi-basement room was provided with a large manger the

Fig. 24

Fig. 29
Plate 12

Fig. 29 Plan of houses at Tarsus. A, courtyard; B, street; C, 'Governor's Residence'; D, ramp with steps; E, harness-room; F, 'manger-room' (after Goldman)

Fig. 30 Section of 'manger-room' area, Tarsus. A, upper living room; B, paved terrace; C, 'manger-room'; D, harness-room; E, ramp; F, street level (after Goldman)

dimensions of which at first suggested to the excavators that it had been used by donkeys. If this is so (the excavators later opted for human occupation[24]) the animals descended by means of a step from the street and crossed a room (a harness-room?) to reach their living-quarters, and the roof of the harness-room was paved with stone to provide a terrace for the inhabitants of the house above the stable. At Beycesultan a considerable area was recognizable as stabling accommodation for horses, complete with mangers, tethering-posts, grooms' quarters and even the remains of straw on the floors.

Fig. 30

Plate 13

If we turn now to the commercial life of these settlements, one- or two-room units opening on to the streets at Alaca have been taken to be shops or workshops, while at Beycesultan there is a fine example of a grain-shop or food-store. This was a rectangular room, about 16 feet by 13 feet, opening directly off a main street. Standing along the walls on either side of the room were large storage-jars, some almost 5 feet in height, which were for the most part about half full of wheat, barley or lentils. In one corner of the room a small stair led up to a sort of 'cat-walk' which ran round the room and gave access to the jars from above. A grain-bin of brick and wood was built against the back wall. For some unexplained reason, a large amount of pottery, some of it nested in matching sets of six, was also found in the room. The proprietors may well have sold crockery as well as grain.

Fig. 31
Plate 14

Immediately behind the grain-store, and approached by a side door, lay a smaller room, about 13 feet by 10 feet, in which the area opposite

ROOM L-II-2.

ROOM L-II-1.
["WINE-SHOP."]

ROOM L-II-3.
["FOOD-STORE"]

SCALE: METRES.

N.

Fig. 31 Wine-shop and food-store at Beycesultan (after Lloyd) the door was largely taken up by a 'bar' of mud-brick, behind which were two storage-jars partly sunk in the floor, and a pile of drinking-cups in one corner. In a large earthenware basin on the customers' side of the bar was a collection of seventy-seven knuckle-bones and thirty-one crescent-shaped terracotta objects which are elsewhere very common and are usually taken to be loom-weights. In this case they had presumably been used in the same way as thrifty card-players of today use matches. Sprawled around the floor were eight human skeletons. From the position of the bones it could be seen that their owners had not, like the Archpoet, simply decided *in taberna mori*, but had been clubbed to death elsewhere and afterwards hurriedly deposited in the room.

Another interesting glimpse of Late Bronze Age catering arrangements is to be seen at Troy, where a building of period VIIa, immediately inside the main South Gate, shows features which suggest that it was something more than a simple dwelling-house. A wide doorway gave access from the street to a small hall-way, off which opened a large room containing a central raised hearth, and beside it a saddle-quern fixed in a tilted position on a stand of crude brick and clay so that flour ground in it would fall into a clay-lined basin in the floor. Against the street-wall was a kitchen sink of stone slabs with a well-built drain which emptied outside the building. Next to the sink were the lower parts of two fire-boxes which had probably originally supported a baking-oven. Next to this, and nearest the city-wall, were storage-bins containing remains of carbonized wheat. All this suggests that the building was used for cooking and food-preparation, and it is a happy fancy of the excavators[25] that a counter was placed across the wide front doorway, and that the establishment was a 'snack-bar' where Trojan heroes, tired by their efforts against the Homeric Greeks, could pause in safety for a beer and a sandwich before reporting to King Priam at the central palace.

Of the palace itself no trace now remains, and we have to turn elsewhere for information on royal residences. The 'Burnt Palace' at Beycesultan dates from the Middle Bronze Age and so is too early to be included in this survey. In the Late Bronze Age the site of this palace was occupied by a walled enclosure about 100 yards across, but the buildings excavated within this area seem domestic in character and already been described in that context. In the south-east, a palace area has been excavated at Tilmen Hüyük, near Islâhiye. This was certainly

Plate 9

Plates 9, 10

used in the Late Bronze Age, but its primary construction took place in the Middle Bronze Age, and once again it is too early for a description to be given here. The same is true of the palaces of central Anatolia which flourished during the Colony-period – Kültepe, Acem Hüyük and Karahuyük-Konya.

Plate 15

This brings us to the most important palace of all, the residence of the rulers of the Hittite Empire, set on the rocky eminence of Büyükkale at Boğazköy. The choice of this hill as a palace-site was an obvious one. It towers above the old city and is protected by sheer cliffs on the eastern and northern sides, while to the south and west it could easily be strengthened by man-made fortifications. The top of the rock forms a sloping roughly trapezoidal plateau about 275 yards by 165 yards in extent. The earliest traces of habitation go back to the end of the third millennium, and by the Colony-period it had acquired a substantial defensive wall of mud brick on a stone foundation. A hundred years after its destruction by Anittas of Kussara it was reoccupied (*c.* 1650 BC) by Hattusilis I, the founder of the Old Kingdom. Unfortunately later building operations have destroyed most of the evidence for structures of this period, and only a few traces of relatively minor buildings have been recovered. About 1400, at the beginning of the Imperial period, there was a considerable amount of rebuilding, most of which is again very poorly preserved. Inside a new defensive wall the lower end of the plateau was occupied by a succession of fairly small free-standing buildings, most of which seem to have been domestic in character. At the upper end, closest to the cliffs and farthest from the gateway at the south-western corner, stood the palace itself. It consisted of a central courtyard surrounded by a colonnade off which the royal apartments opened. Other buildings were erected round the edge of the plateau, and since the area available was too small to support the rising aspirations of the Hittite monarchy it was extended on the east and west sides by the addition of huge terraces of cyclopean boulders on which the foundation of the walls and outer buildings rested. Unfortunately most of the details have again been destroyed by later building operations.

Just before 1300 BC Muwatallis transferred the seat of government further south to Datassa, and Hattusas became for a short time a mere provincial capital. To this period may be dated the modest domestic buildings on the lower plateau known as level IVa. Later, under

Urhi-Teshub, the palace was at least partly destroyed, and his successor Hattusilis III seized the opportunity for a large-scale reconstruction which was not completed until the reign of Tudhaliyas IV. This is Büyükkale III, sufficient of which has been preserved to give a reasonably good picture of the thirteenth-century palace of the Hittite kings.

Fig. 32

During this period the palace buildings were extended to fill the whole of the plateau. In order to make the maximum use of the space available the rock-terraces of the previous period were reserved for building purposes and new defensive walls were founded on extremely difficult ground further down the steep slopes. The main public entrance to the citadel was still at the south-west corner. It had, like the city gates, two doorways and outside flanking towers, and was reached by means of a fairly narrow ramp suitable only for pedestrian traffic. Once inside the gate, the visitor found himself in an entrance-court of irregular shape across which a path of red marble slabs led through a portal to a larger court; long, open colonnades formed three sides of this, uniting the individual buildings round the court into a single architectural unit. On the far side was another gateway, an elaborate triple structure with guard-rooms or porters' cubicles on either side. This led to a further courtyard where again open colonnades linked the façades of imposing buildings. Beyond this lay yet another similar court round which, on the highest and most spectacular part of the site, lay the residential quarters of the royal family.

The king himself did not need to use the public entrance. He could leave the middle courtyard by a door or gate at its south-eastern corner, and proceed from there by way of a second gate in the citadel-wall provided with an outer ramp with a width and gradient suitable for chariots. For the benefit of servants and minor officials who lived in the lower town there was a third entrance, a much less grandiose structure which led via a ramp or staircase from the southern end of the western wall to the terraces behind the main palace-buildings. Finally a paved road ran along the inside of the southern wall between the two main gateways. This road could be closed at two points by doorways, and although the paving suggests something of greater importance, it must have been a mere short-cut for palace functionaries.

When we turn to the purpose for which individual buildings in the palace-complex were built our path is beset with difficulties. The

Fig. 32 Plan of Büyükkale, the citadel of Hattusas (Boğazköy) (after Bittel)

sloping nature of the site, for instance, is such that buildings were entered from the courtyards at first-floor level, so that surviving walls give us only the plans of basement rooms. Worse than this, some of the most important buildings on the highest part of the rock have been so completely destroyed by later clearances that only very slight traces of them remain. Of the structures to the east of the middle courtyard, for instance, virtually nothing survives, while in the innermost court only the barest traces, such as beddings for the bases of the pillars of the colonnade, cut into the bare rock of the plateau, give an indication of what must once have stood there.

A part from these difficulties the function of even well-preserved buildings is often more or less impossible to determine. But in some instances sufficient evidence survives to permit reasonable guesses to be made. The two buildings west of the upper courtyard (Buildings E and F) are almost certainly domestic in character. The building to the south of the middle courtyard (Building A) contained large numbers of clay tablets, and presumably housed the royal archive and library. Other tablets were found in Buildings E and K, but it has been suggested that the library was temporarily split up because of the continuing process of rebuilding.[26] Building D, on the western side of the same court, has a

Fig. 33

Fig. 33 Plan of Building D, Büyükkale (after Akurgal)

basement level which consists almost entirely of long narrow rooms. The walls of these may well have served as supports for rows of pillars at courtyard level. These pillars in their turn would have supported an upper storey and formed the principal feature of an audience-hall over 100 feet square. This hall could be entered either directly from the middle courtyard or via a narrow lane which led through a door from the north-western corner of the lower courtyard to a side entrance at basement level. From this entrance a staircase brought visitors to the vestibule of the hall, and so into the royal presence, without the need for them to enter the middle court.

Not all the buildings in the palace complex were for secular use. Building C, which lay rather off the beaten track towards the western edge of the plateau, may well have had a ritual purpose. More will be said of this in the chapter on religion.

At Alaca, only a few miles north of Boğazköy, the largest building has several features which are sufficiently reminiscent of the structures in Büyükkale for it to be claimed as a palace. The entrance to this building faces the main city-gate across a wide open square, and leads by way of an outer court and a double gateway to a long, narrow courtyard some 250 feet by 50 feet in extent. At the centre of the right-hand side of this court is an open colonnade, and the pattern of the pillars is picked up and emphasized by means of pilasters on at least some of the walls on either side of the court. The principal room lies just to the right of the double gateway, and is entered by way of two narrower rooms from a door at the southern end of the colonnade. Its size, about 40 feet square,

Figs. 21, 34

Fig. 34 Reconstruction of the east side of the palace at Alaca (after Koşay and Akok)

suggests that if it was roofed (and its position next to the main court makes it unlikely that it was also a courtyard) the roof would have needed internal support, making this another 'pillar-hall' like the one in Büyükkale. Other rooms are presumably domestic or administrative in character, and one, at the north-western corner, may have been a shrine.

The everyday life of most ordinary citizens of second-millennium Anatolia was concerned almost exclusively with agriculture. Although not enough work has been done on the ecology of the area, sufficient is known from textual and archaeological sources to give a fairly clear picture of the fauna and flora both wild and domesticated. The main crops were emmer-wheat and barley; but peas, beans, onions, flax, figs, olives, grapes, apples and possibly pears and pomegranates also were grown. Cattle, pigs, goats, sheep, horses, donkeys, dogs and perhaps water-buffalo were kept, and bees too were an important item. Wild animals included lion, leopard, wolf, deer, hare, wild bull, wild boar, wild goat, eagle, dove, duck, snake and mouse. Daily diet consisted mainly of different sorts of bread and cakes, milk, cheese, porridge or gruel, and meat and vegetable stews. Agricultural implements have been found at various sites, and a glance through a dictionary provides words for farm, sheepfold, pig-sty, goat-pen, stable, threshing-floor, woodshed, orchard, meadow, beehive, granary, millstone, water-trough, plough, spade, cart and harness. In other words, the peasant's life was little different from that of his contemporaries anywhere in the Aegean-Middle Eastern world, and remarkably similar to that of his descendants in present-day Turkey.

Plate 16

The importance of agricultural production to the Hittite state can easily be seen if we consider the vast amount of food that was necessary to supply a city as big as Hattusas, not to mention the other towns of the realm. Estimates of population are notoriously inaccurate, but the capital covered an area of 414 acres, and if even half of this was occupied by houses the standard average of 150–200 persons per acre gives a figure of about 30,000–40,000 inhabitants. Since it has been calculated that the 'consumption-yield' of grain under Bronze Age agricultural conditions was about seven bushels per acre, and that annual grain-consumption under these conditions is about ten bushels per head per annum, the annual consumption of the citizens of Hattusas must have been 300,000–

400,000 bushels, the produce of between 40,000 and 60,000 acres of corn-land. Most of this must have been grown in the fertile agricultural land immediately north of the city.

Fig. 35

Farming, however, was not the only livelihood available. There is evidence for the presence of doctors, builders, carpenters, stonemasons, goldsmiths, coppersmiths, potters, bakers, shoemakers, weavers, tailors, fullers, tavern-keepers (male and female), fishermen, cooks, porters and watchmen, although in many cases full-time professionals were employed only by the palace and temples. Sometimes there is evidence for what can only be described as industrial areas, especially in connection with metalworking. This was partly done at the mines, and despite the importance of Anatolia as a metal-source the evidence, in the shape of workings and slag-heaps, is by no means as clear as it is, say, in Cyprus. Metal was transported from the mines in the form of ingots, and the best examples are again Cypriot in origin, but were found in the wreck of a Syrian vessel off the south Turkish coast. The final shaping into tools and weapons was done locally, and areas devoted to this have been found at Boğazköy and Tarsus marked by the presence of large quantities of slag. Tarsus also produced part of a clay crucible with bronze still adhering to it.

Fig. 35 Knife from Troy; spindle-whorl from Kusura; loom-weight from Troy; nails from Alaca; spindle-whorl from Polatli; loom-weight from Alaca; knife from Kusura. Not to scale

Fig. 36 Suggested reconstruction of monument at Eflatun Pinar, with Fassilar figure top left (after Mellaart)

Stone-carving seems to have been organized on the same lines as metalworking, with preliminary shaping being done at the quarry and the final touches being given once the statue was in position. At Yesemek, south-east of Islâhiye, literally hundreds of half-finished statues, dating to the last quarter of the second millennium and the first quarter of the first, are to be seen lying around waiting for transportation, while the colossal figure abandoned on the hillside at Fassilar, near Lake Beyşehir, may well have been on its way to its final position at the spring sanctuary of Eflatun Pinar, some 30 miles away.

An area devoted to the making of pottery has recently been excavated at Eskiyapar, near Alaca. In the Hittite level of this site was an open

Fig. 36
Plate 32

courtyard in which were situated two round kilns, each about 5 feet in diameter, with a central post and radiating struts for the floor of the upper chamber. Water was supplied through terracotta pipes, and fragments of unfired and misfired plates were recovered. Similar establishments were doubtless situated in many Hittite towns.

Other industries were more domestic in character. Spinning and weaving were done at home, as can be seen from the large numbers of *Fig. 35* spindle-whorls and loom-weights which have survived at many sites. That older industries also survived can be seen in a room at Kültepe which contained a large amount of worked obsidian, stored presumably for future use in such implements as threshing-sledges.

The normal everyday clothing for the average Hittite was a knee-length, shirt-like tunic, rather inelegantly known as the 'garment with the neck coming out'. It had long sleeves and was usually worn without *Fig. 37* a belt. A longer and more luxurious version, called a 'Hurrian shirt', was worn on festive occasions. It could be trimmed with coloured embroidery or metal decorations, and was sometimes worn with an ornamental belt or waist-band. The light tunic with a kilt, frequently to be seen on monuments, was probably military equipment for light mobile troops, and the long gown or mantle, likewise carved on the monuments, was normally worn by gods, kings and priests for religious ceremonies. Kings and priests also had round caps or head-bands, but

Fig. 37 'Hurrian shirt' from an Egyptian relief (after Pritchard)

these can be seen also on the hunters and acrobats of the Alaca reliefs. Plate 55
The high conical hat, a symbol of divinity, may also have been worn by
the king on important state occasions. Shoes or boots with upturned
toes were made in different colours and ornamented in various ways.
Stockings or gaiters were also worn. The normal outdoor dress for
women was a long cloak which enveloped the figure from head to foot.
Beneath this was a lighter garment for use in the privacy of the house.
The long pleated skirt, broad belt and high *polos* hat of the goddess at Plate 46
Yazilikaya seem to have been reserved primarily for divinities, but the
queen may sometimes have worn them in her capacity as high priestess.

Clothing was normally fastened by one or two ornamental bronze
pins at the shoulders. Hair was usually worn long, hanging over
the neck and shoulders or arranged in a pig tail. Men were clean shaven.
Jewellery was worn by both sexes, and there are examples of ear rings, Plate 17
bracelets and necklaces. Hanging pendants, probably with some sort of Fig. 38
amuletic function, were popular – ornamental 'sun discs', lunate Plates 18–20
shapes, pairs of shoes and animal or divine figurines, singly or in groups.
Finger rings are also known. One particularly fine example was

*Fig. 38 Child's bracelet, probably from Western Turkey, now in the British Museum
(No. 132116)*

Figs. 39, 40

designed to be used as a seal, but the signet-ring, like the cylinder-seal, was the exception in the Hittite world. The normal form was the stamp-seal, usually of a conical shape rising from a circular base to a ring or perforated boss by means of which it was suspended from a cord. Lens-shaped seals are also found. These have a design on each side, and are pivoted in a U-shaped metal holder for ease of use. Seals of the early Old Hittite period were a direct continuation of those of the later Colony-period. The principal motif could be purely geometric, or could take the form of an eagle, a griffin, a quadruped, a human figure, or occasion-ally several figures combined. Sometimes decoration was added round the border of the seal. Many of these motifs disappeared during the course of the Old Kingdom, and it was also during this period that writing was first introduced into the designs. This was in the form of 'Hittite Hieroglyphs', which replaced the central motif within the decorated border. Among the names which can be read, those ending in -muwa and -ziti predominate, and since these are known to be Luwian in origin a strong Old Kingdom Luwian element in the population seems probable. Occasionally there is a combination of hieroglyphs with cuneiform writing.

Fig. 40

From the time of Telepinus (*c.* 1500) onward there is an increasing number of so-called '*tabarna*-seals', and these become the characteristic royal seals of the Middle Kingdom. They consist of a small central area with ornamentation or hieroglyphs surrounded by a two-line cuneiform inscription containing the royal title *tabarna*, but almost never the name of its bearer. Parallel to these are '*tawananna*-seals' belong-ing to queens. On them, for some unknown reason, the central sign is in cuneiform rather than hieroglyphic Hittite.

By about 1400 royal seals were beginning to acquire the characteristics of the Imperial period. Foremost among these is the *aedicula*, the winged sun-disc extended above the hieroglyphic name (or sometimes title) in the central area of the seals. The cuneiform legend gives the name, titles and sometimes ancestry of the monarch, and in some cases also of his queen. In the finest and most elaborate seals (first apparently in the reign of Muwatallis) the central area shows the king in the embrace of his protective deity. These seals were used in communications with foreign powers and for giving the royal assent to treaties, and represent the highest point of Hittite glyptic art. Seals of lesser mortals during the Imperial

Fig. 39 Seal-impressions. Top row, l. from Boğazköy; centre from Ugarit; r. from Boğazköy. Bottom row, l. from Boğazköy; centre and r. from Ugarit

Fig. 40 Impressions of royal seals. Top row, l. Huzziyas; centre Asmunikkal; r. Mursilis II. Bottom row, l. Arnuwandas and Asmunikkal; centre Hattusilis III and Puduhepa; r. Muwatallis period continued the tradition of a hieroglyphic inscription within a circular border. In some cases the central inscription is accompanied by a figure – divine, human or animal – and in others the border becomes an elaborate arrangement of pictorial motifs, or even of triangular marks which seem deliberately designed to give a casual observer the impression of a royal seal with a cuneiform inscription round the edge.

Finally, some description must be given of the pottery of Late Bronze Age Anatolia. Needless to say, there was no one pottery-style prevalent over the whole area, and several different pottery-provinces can be distinguished. Pottery of 'Hittite' type was in use throughout central Anatolia and in many areas affected by Hittite political or military

Fig. 41

Fig. 41 Boğazköy; typical pottery shapes (after Fischer)

influence. It is predominantly monochrome, and ranges from brown through reddish-brown to red. For the most part it carries on the earlier tradition of the central area, but there is a distinct falling-off in ceramic achievement, perhaps to be associated with 'mass-production' techniques.[27] Characteristic shapes among pouring vessels are the beak-spouted jug (now slimmer and less elegant than its predecessor in the Colony-period), the 'tea-pot', a jug with narrow round neck and handle from neck to shoulder, and the lentoid flask with one or three handles. Cups are rare, but bowls are found in many shapes, some with simple rounded profile and rounded rim, others with rims which show thickening on the outside or (especially in the thirteenth century) on the inside. Carinated bowls are less common, but found in all periods, and under the later Empire a plate with a wide rim is especially frequent. At this time too bowls with handles are more common than they were in earlier periods. Miniature vessels, presumably votive in purpose, are also to be found, and 'spindle-bottles' and 'libation-arms', the immediate connections of which are with north Syria and Cyprus, are indications of ceramic influence from the south-east. Characteristic of the central area is a rare type of pottery with decoration in moulded relief. Polychrome vessels bearing ritual scenes, such as that from Bitik and a recently discovered example from Inandik, are probably of Old Kingdom date, and monochrome examples, known only from fragments, are to be dated to the Imperial period.

Plate 21

Perhaps the most attractive type of Hittite pottery is the vessel in the form of an animal. Lion-figures are known, but bulls are much more common, and birds, especially water-birds, also occur. The prize specimens of this type are the two large bull-vessels, each nearly 3 feet tall, found in an early Imperial context on the lower part of the citadel

Fig. 42

Plate 22

Fig. 42 Vase in the form of a two-headed duck, from Boğazköy. H. 8 in.

terrace at Boğazköy. Their surfaces are coated with a highly polished red slip, and they have cream-painted patches on their foreheads, shoulders and haunches. Each also has inlaid black eyeballs, a white-painted halter attached to a nose-ring, an opening at the base of the neck to enable liquid to be poured in, and two open nostrils for pouring it out again. That the vessels were designed to form a pair can be deducted from the way their tails hang. They have been identified with Sheri and Hurri, the bulls of the Weather-god in Hurrian and Imperial Hittite cult.

Pottery of Hittite type is found as far west as the Eskişehir area. This may well represent a measure of political domination (the area has been identified with Wilusa), but the same cannot be true of northern Anatolia, although 'Hittite' pottery has been found around Kastamonu, Eflani, Ilgaz and Gerede, as well as in the area immediately north of Hattusas at Horoztepe and at Dundartepe on the Black Sea coast near Samsun. The pottery of this area, although recognizably derivative, in some ways preserves the finer traditions of the Colony-period to a greater extent than does that of central Anatolia. Clearly the Gasga-peoples, although they tended to absorb much of Hittite cultures, in some ways at least achieved a higher standard than their southern neighbours.

Another area which reflects Hittite political domination in its ceramic repertoire is Cilicia. Here too there are to be found shallow bowls or plates, lentoid flasks, narrow-necked jugs and other central Anatolian forms. In the Elazığ area also the Hittite presence can be detected in the pottery. Here grey wares which belong to an earlier local tradition are accompanied by vessels of Old Kingdom type. These are followed by characteristic Imperial forms, especially coarse plates, mostly in an orange ware as opposed to central Anatolian brown or red.

Elsewhere in eastern Anatolia ceramic evidence for the Late Bronze Age is almost non-existent. It has been suggested that after a flourishing period in the third millennium the area lapsed into nomadism for much of the second,[28] but this can only be substantiated through further research and excavation.

If we now turn to western Anatolia we move into a different ceramic world. The north-west, for instance, has its own range of shapes and fabrics, best known from Troy (late VI and VIIa), but found also down the coast as far as Smyrna, on the off-shore islands, and inland on the

Fig. 43

Fig. 43 Typical pottery shapes of north-west Anatolia (after Blegen)

plains of Balikesir and Akhisar-Manisa. The most distinctive pottery of
the area is of fine quality and finished with a burnished grey slip, the
'Grey Minyan' of the publications on Troy. This is never the only
pottery in use, being invariably accompanied by red or buff wares. At
Troy, for instance, red ware is common in the earlier stages of level VI,
but then disappears, and buff wares are characteristic of late VI and
VIIa. At Smyrna, on the other hand, grey ware appears late and becomes the principal ware only in the Late Bronze Age. The pottery of
the whole area, with its high handles, sharp carinations and rivet-
shaped knobs, strongly suggests the existence of metallic prototypes, and
it has been suggested that the grey, red and buff wares are imitations of
silver, gold and copper.[29] Central Anatolian shapes such as the beak-
spouted jug and the wide-rimmed plate are conspicuously lacking.
Characteristic forms are bowls with straight sides, with or without a
foot, carinated bowls with everted rims and often with rising handles,
delicate rounded bowls, round-mouthed and trefoil-mouthed jugs,
lentoid flasks, and various types of wide-mouthed jar. Decoration is
largely limited to incised wavy lines, especially on the shoulders of pots,
with a few raised ridges, swellings and knobs. The only exotic feature is a

Fig. 44   liking at Troy for handles in the form of animal-heads. At Troy too
there is abundant evidence for the import of Mycenaean pottery and for
imitation of Mycenaean shapes by local potters. Elsewhere in the area

Fig. 44 Handles in the form of animal-heads, from Troy VI (after Blegen)

Mycenaean influence is negligible, although there are signs that imports reached as far inland as Sardis and even beyond.

The area around Iznik seems, on the evidence of surface survey, to constitute a separate pottery-province, characterized by orange-buff burnished wares with frequent pattern-burnishing, accompanied by unburnished buff vessels which may represent a simpler form of the burnished ware. Without the evidence of excavation it is difficult to date these wares with any precision.

The Late Bronze Age in south-western Anatolia, best represented by levels III, II and I at Beycesultan, is marked by yet a different and distinctive type of pottery. In level III vessels with a dark brown wash survive from the Middle Bronze Age, but most pottery of this level has

Fig. 45
Plate 23

Fig. 45 Beycesultan : typical pottery shapes (after Mellaart)

a polished red or buff slip. There is also a lustrous ware in red, grey or gold with a micaceous polished wash. This 'imitation metal ware' becomes by far the most popular fabric of level II, although it is still accompanied by some burnished wares. In level I many features of level II survive, but these are gradually replaced by a new slipped ware in a range of distinctive colours – off-white, orange, pink, plum-red and others – and by a coarse kitchen-ware decorated with rope-impressions. The most characteristic south-western shapes are a variety of chalices and 'fruit-stands', one-handled 'beer-mugs', carinated bowls, usually without handles, flat-rimmed plates, bifoil- and trefoil-mouthed jugs, jugs with elongated 'bearded' beak-spouts, and large and small *askoi* which must reflect Aegean influence. A curious vessel peculiar to level II is the 'drink-warmer', a two-handled vessel divided horizontally into two compartments. The upper of these is bowl-shaped, while the lower is provided with an opening through which charcoal could be inserted and with ventilation-holes to provide a draught. No contem-porary parallels for these vessels are known.

The Late Bronze Age ceramic material in the south-west forms a fairly homogeneous whole until the introduction in level I of foreign features, most of which seem to have their origin in central Anatolia. These were at first taken to be signs of a refugee element which arrived in the south-west after the destruction of the Hittite Empire, but a detailed ceramic comparison suggests that the central features at Beycesultan are to be dated to the thirteenth rather than the twelfth century. No convinc-ing historical reason for their appearance at that time has so far been suggested.

Some scholars, it should be added here, have suggested that the Late Bronze Age material from Beycesultan has so many parallels in the central Anatolian Middle Bronze Age that it should in fact be dated to that period rather than to the later second millennium. On the whole, the evidence available seems to the author to favour a Late Bronze Age date, but the final publication of the material should help to resolve the problem.

There remains only the question of Mycenaean pottery in south-western Anatolia. Excavations of settlements and graveyards at Miletus, Iasos and Müsgebi have left little doubt that there was genuine Mycen-aean occupation on the southern part of the west coast. On other parts of the coast settlement was non-existent, and inland penetration was minimal. Many regard the fortified towns of Miletus and Iasos as sufficient proof of the existence in that area of the kingdom known to the Hittites as Ahhiyawa. This is a theory which has many attractions, but as far as the author is concerned it causes historical and geographical difficulties which cannot be ignored. It is because of these difficulties that Ahhiyawa appears on the map in this volume in the north-western corner of Anatolia.

CHAPTER V
Warfare and Defence

The military and diplomatic problems which the Hittites faced in maintaining themselves were caused primarily by their geographical position and their economic needs. In order to understand these problems more fully it is necessary to look in some detail at the land of Hatti and its relations with neighbouring countries. Our starting-point may well be the city of Hattusas itself, and its situation on a rocky ridge looking north across a fertile plain turns our attention immediately in that direction. This rich agricultural land supplied much of the capital's corn, and its defence against the Gasga from the northern hills was a perpetual problem for the Hittite authorities. No permanent Gasgan conquest of the area was necessary; a yearly destruction of the crops was sufficient to disrupt the life of the capital. To prevent these annual raids some sort of frontier-line had to be established and maintained, and this was a constant preoccupation of Hittite kings throughout the period of the Empire. The strategic centre of this area was Hakpis (probably present-day Amasya), and from this town a line of fortified posts extended through such places as Hanhana and Hattena (perhaps near Merzifon and Gumushaciköy) in the direction of the holy city of Nerik, most probably situated near the sharp bend of the Halys opposite Kargi.[30] Nerik itself was dangerously close to Gasgan territory, and was for a long period in Gasgan hands. The strength of the northern frontier depended on constant patrolling between the fortified positions, and on the use of local inhabitants to spy and report on Gasgan movements. If the line broke, a last-ditch defence along a line running from Amasya through Çorum was possible. If this too fell, there was nothing to prevent a Gasgan descent on the capital itself.

Immediately east of Hakpis the frontier ran, probably through the narrow gorge of the Yeşil Irmak, to Gaziura at present-day Turhal. From there it continued until it reached the upper Halys somewhere between Sivas and Zara. Along this line too there was constant raiding

Plate 15

by Gasga tribesmen, and although Hittite forces penetrated as far as the river Kummesmaha (possibly the Kelkit Çay) they were unable to gain any permanent advantage. Gasgan armies were able not only to devastate the area north of the Halys, but on occasion to cross the river and sweep down its southern bank towards Kanesh, near modern Kayseri, thus endangering the Hittites' most important communication-route with the east.

Somewhere in the hills east of Zara the Gasga-lands ended and the land of Azzi-Hayasa began. This country must have controlled the rich metal-deposits of north-eastern Anatolia, and although Suppiluliu-mas attempted to win access to these by diplomacy and Mursilis tried to gain the same end by force, there is little indication that the Hittites gained any permanent footing in this area. They were able only to hold a frontier-line from the upper Halys to the Euphrates. Behind this line lay the buffer-province known as the Upper Land, with its administra-tive and religious centre at Samuha. This town has been placed by some scholars on the Halys, and by others on the Euphrates.[31] It may, in the author's opinion, have been situated at or near present-day Divriği. Strategically the Upper Land was extremely important, for if it fell it exposed to enemy attack the road from Sivas (perhaps Hittite Marassan-tiya) to the plain of Malatya (perhaps Hittite Tegarama), a road which was always an important Hittite route to northern Syria, and which indeed from the days of Mursilis I until the time of Suppiluliumas provided their only means of communication with that area.

Across the Euphrates from the Malatya plain was the land of Isuwa, within whose boundaries lay the Ergani Maden, the richest copper-source in the Middle East. Its situation between Hatti and Mitanni made it a constant source of contention between these powers, and again it was Suppiluliumas who secured the area in Hittite hands. From then until its loss to Assyria in the reign of Tudhaliyas IV (*c.* 1265 BC) the re-sources of Isuwa were available for the equipping of Hittite armies.

The importance of the routes which lead from central Anatolia to northern Syria has already been sufficiently stressed. Apart from the Sivas-Malatya road, mentioned above, the principal routes were those which led from Kanesh (near modern Kayseri) through the passes of the Anti-Taurus mountains, the famous 'Cilician Gates' opening on to the plain of Cilicia, and the route which led down from the southern plateau at modern Karaman to the Mediterranean coast at Silifke and thence along the coast via Mersin, Tarsus and Adana. In the days before the rise of Hittite power Assyrian merchants had made full use of the Anti-Taurus passes, and the early Hittite monarch Hattusilis I (*c.* 1650) seems to have controlled both these routes and the Cilician Gates. But by the time of Telepinus (*c.* 1500) Cilicia had become the independent land of Adaniya, centred presumably on modern Adana, while the more northerly routes were included in the land of Kizzu-wadna, a kingdom whose capital Kummani probably lay somewhere in the neighbourhood of modern Şar. An alliance with Kizzuwadna enabled Telepinus to make use of these routes, but shortly afterwards the rising power of Mitanni wooed Kizzuwadna from her allegiance to the Hittites. After that, control of the Anti-Taurus area frequently changed hands as the rival powers strove to assert their authority, and it seems that during this confused period Kizzuwadna managed to absorb Adaniya, thus giving her control of the Cilician Gates and the Karaman-Silifke road as well as the more northerly routes. Eventually Suppiluliumas was able to conclude a firm treaty with Kizzuwadna by which that country was left in control of the southerly routes while the Anti-Taurus area was fully incorporated into the land of Hatti. Under Mursilis Cilicia too was absorbed, with the result that when Muwatallis had to face the challenge of Egypt he could move his capital to Datassa, a town somewhere in the region of the Karaman-Silifke route, in part at least because it was down that route that his contingents from western Anatolia would pass to Cilicia and so to northern Syria.

With the absorption of Kizzuwadna the boundaries of the Hittites were extended beyond their mountain homeland into the area between the Mediterranean and the Euphrates. Here the principal power had long been Aleppo, the old enemy of Hattusilis I and Mursilis I, and after his Syrian victories Suppiluliumas was quick to place his son on the throne of that town. But at the same time he had another son crowned as king of Aleppo's great rival Carchemish, and from then on it was Hittite policy to encourage the leadership of Carchemish at the expense of Aleppo. Around this bastion on the Euphrates were arranged several vassal-kingdoms, including a reorganized Mitanni to face Assyria, Ugarit and Alalah on the Mediterranean coast, and Kinza (Qadesh) and Amurru to the south to block the routes by which Egypt might seek to assert her power. This was an arrangement which held good until the final years of the Hittite Empire.

A good deal has been said in an earlier chapter about Hittite policy in dealing with the south-west and west. Here the natural boundary was the western edge of the Konya Plain (the Hittite 'Lower Land'), and beyond this line lay the Arzawa lands. Here, as on the Gasgan frontier, a strong fortress-line was necessary, for despite several conquests of Arzawa and the creation of buffer-kingdoms in Hapalla (around Lakes Beyşehir and Eğridir) and Mira (the Afyon-Kütahya area) there was no permanent consolidation of Hittite power in the west. Further north lay the second great Hittite life-line, the route to the Sea of Marmara and the Troad. Along this route a policy of diplomatic tact was usually followed, for on the whole states like Ahhiyawa (the Troad?) and Wilusa (the plain of Eskişehir?) realized that a continuous flow of trade was to their advantage. What was necessary was the protection of the route from attack by the Arzawa lands, and it was for this purpose that the Seha River Land (around Balikesir?) was maintained and given special privileges as a buffer-state against aggression from the south.

To the north of the route lay the lands of the River Hulana (around Beypazari), Kassiya (the valley of the Devrez Çay), and Pala and Tummana (around Kastamonu). It was the policy of Hittite monarchs to maintain these centres as a defence against the peoples further north towards the Black Sea coast. Here the country was really a continuation of the Gasga-lands, and no permanent conquest was ever effected. The kingdoms of Masa (around Bolu) and Arawanna (perhaps Safranbolu) were a constant danger to the more westerly areas, while Tummana and Pala, situated just west of the lower Halys, were an open target for Gasgan attack. As on the rest of the Gasga frontier, the only possible policy was one of constant vigilance and counter-attack.

On a frontier as long and diverse as the one just described no single policy was likely to be applicable to all problems. In an ideal world where resources are plentiful and trade flows freely both producers and consumers realize their mutual dependence, firm agreements are reached, and frontiers virtually cease to exist. But the Anatolian world was far from ideal. All round the Hittite homeland were other powers competing for the same resources, and it was the defence of these resources, or of the routes leading to them, that dictated Hittite policy. Alliances between the great powers were possible only when two of them were faced by a threat from a third (as when Hatti and Egypt united against Assyria). Apart from this, international diplomacy was unlikely to have much success.

In this competitive world the Hittites had the great advantage of being an inland 'continental' power. Although they had enemies on all sides, it was unlikely that these enemies would act in unison, and in their central position the Hittites could quickly move their armies from one frontier to another as dangerous situations developed. Sometimes attempts were made to solve frontier-problems by conquest (the invasion of Mitanni by Suppiluliumas, and of the Arzawa-Lands by Mursilis are cases in point), but on the whole, Hittite kings realized that control of what they had was enough to ensure their superiority. The maintenance of this control depended, as we have seen, on two main policies, diplomatic arrangements with minor buffer-states, and the use of military force.

Hittite diplomacy will be dealt with in another chapter. Here our concern must be with the army which played such a large part in Hittite history. This army, which on occasions numbered up to 30,000 men, consisted of two main arms, infantry and chariots. The infantry had a small core of permanent troops who acted as the king's personal body-guard and were responsible for frontier-patrols and the crushing of rebellions. Nothing is known of their recruitment, but they were at times supplemented by foreign mercenary troops. During the cam-paigning-seasons a larger infantry-force was raised from the local popula-tion and if necessary it was further enlarged by contingents from vassal-kingdoms. There were also pioneers for siege-work and messengers who may in some cases have been mounted. Apart from this, the horse was used only to draw the chariot – the principal offensive weapon of the Hittites, as of all other contemporary Near Eastern powers.

The supreme commander was the king himself, and it is clear that Hittite kings took a prominent personal part in any fighting in which their armies were involved. On occasion command could be delegated, if for instance the king were ill, or engaged in a campaign elsewhere, or if his presence were needed for cult-duties at home. In such cases the delegated commander would normally be a member of the royal family, and would bear some high-sounding court-title such as Chief Shepherd or Master of the Wine. In some areas (for instance the northern frontier and the Euphrates line at Carchemish) special attention was necessary at all times. In such a case a royal prince could be given the title of 'king' of the area and granted a more-or-less independent command.

The system of ranks in the Hittite army is difficult to reconstruct, but it seems that minor commands were held by the lesser nobility, and that units were built up as a decimal system with officers in charge of ten, one hundred and one thousand men in a rising hierarchy of command.

Equally little is known about the payment of troops. In many cases military service was a feudal obligation and thus part of a wider system of which more will be said in another chapter. In addition, the Hittites believed in payment by results, and victory in the field was regularly followed by the distribution of booty. The dangers of this system can be seen at the Battle of Qadesh, where an easy Hittite victory was almost turned to defeat by the anxiety of the chariot troops to plunder the enemy camp before ensuring that the field was fully theirs.

Troops in enemy territory doubtless lived off the land. The garrisons of border fortresses were presumably supported by the local population, and the same may be true of the large contingents which were frequently moved from one end to the other of the Hittite realms. But Hittite armies also had large baggage trains of donkeys and bullock carts which must have carried supplies as well as equipment. The principal problem both in Anatolia and in northern Syria must have been that of water supply, and in many areas the number of routes which could have been used even by small forces is closely limited by the availability of this essential commodity.

In considering the equipment of Hittite armies we may well start from a recent definition of the art of warfare as an attempt 'to achieve supremacy over the enemy in three fields: mobility, fire power, security'.[32] In the first field the principal weapon of the Hittites, as of the other powers of the time, was the light horse drawn chariot. This vehicle was developed in a Hurrian milieu about the middle of the second millennium, and its use rapidly spread through the Middle East. The perfected chariot was a remarkably skilful piece of work, light in weight and extremely manoeuvrable at speed. The body consisted of a wooden frame covered with leather. This was mounted on a wide axle on which ran spoked wooden wheels. A pole ran forward from the underside of the body, on either side of which a horse was yoked. The

Fig. 46

Fig. 46 Hittite chariot in action.
From an Egyptian relief in the
Ramesseum, Thebes (after
Yadin)

superiority of the Hittites in chariot-warfare lay not in their possession
of this weapon (all their enemies had it too) but in their variation of the
basic pattern to suit their own purposes. The ultimate problem in
chariot-design is to reconcile speed and manoeuvrability with fire-power
and security. For the former the designer must concentrate on lightness
and such problems as the length and position of the axle; for the latter
he must make his vehicle sufficiently steady for weapons to be used from
it, and either give it a body which will afford some kind of protection or
evolve some other means by which the warrior can protect himself. In
other words, he must recognize that a charioteer has a triple function;
he has simultaneously to control his chariot, fight an offensive battle, and
defend himself. One answer to all this is the method adopted by Egyptian

Plate 5

pharaohs. Rameses II at Qadesh, for instance, can be seen clad in a coat
of mail for protection, and he has the reins tied round his waist to leave
both hands free to operate his bow. A javelin-case is attached to the side
of his chariot which, like all Egyptian chariots of the period, has its axle
at the rear of the body, a position making for maximum manoeuvrability at speed. Lesser Egyptians did not share the pharaoh's all-round
skill, and the normal Egyptian battle-chariot had a crew of two, a driver
and a warrior armed with a bow and javelins. Clearly the Egyptians
regarded chariots as highly mobile firing-platforms from which long-
and medium-range missiles could be dispatched in a manner which
would cause the maximum of confusion in the enemy ranks. The
Hittite conception of chariot-warfare was different from this. To them a
chariot formation was a heavy-weight assault force which could sweep
through and demolish infantry-lines in an organized charge. So we find

Fig. 46

that in Hittite chariots the principal weapon employed was the stabbing-

98

spear for action at close range, and that the axle was attached to the middle of the body rather than the rear. This meant that their vehicles were more liable to overturn at speed, but the sacrifice in manoeuvrability was more than counterbalanced by the increase in fire-power which resulted from it. For, because of the forward mounting of the wheels, the Hittite chariot could carry a crew of three – a driver, a warrior and a soldier who during the charge held a shield to protect the other two. Thus extra weight was given to the charge and extra man-power was available in the hand-to-hand fighting which followed it.

Other Anatolian powers, such as Arzawa, Ahhiyawa and even the Gasga-lands, had their chariot-forces too, but apart from references to them in Hittite texts nothing is known of their composition or arma-ment. Indeed, much of Anatolia is such difficult country that chariots cannot have been of much assistance in battle, and they may have been used mainly for the rapid transport of kings and high-ranking officials – and for their rapid escape after a defeat, if we may judge by the number of Hittite enemies who 'fled alone', leaving their troops, and even their wives and children, to the tender mercies of the Great King.

Much less is known about the infantry divisions of the Hittite army. At the Battle of Qadesh they played a very minor part, being used mainly to protect the baggage and equipment against sudden enemy attack. But in the Anatolian hills the infantryman came into his own, and in this type of fighting too, if we can judge from the admittedly biased royal records, the Hittite army had the advantage of its opponents. This advantage seems to have been gained not so much by superior fire-power as by better training and discipline, which enabled Hittite generals to move their troops over large distances making full use of the cover of natural features or of darkness, and so to achieve the element of surprise which could be so important in a successful attack. When the attack came, the marching column could quickly be turned into a battle-line which could sweep through an enemy army before it had time to organize itself. Some of the effect of the rapidly advancing Hittite line may be seen in the controlled and sinister movement of the warrior-gods in the sculpture-gallery at Yazilikaya.

Plate 51

The principal offensive weapon of the Hittite infantryman seems to have varied according to the nature of the terrain. In northern Syria, where set battles in open country were a possibility, he was armed with a

Fig. 47 Weapons. Socketed spearhead from Beycesultan; tang-and-button spearhead (Middle Bronze Age) of unknown provenance; straight sword from an Egyptian relief at Medinet Habu; sickle-sword from a relief at Yazilikaya; arrowhead from Boğazköy; shaft-hole axe from Boğazköy. Not to scale

Plate 24
Fig. 47
Plate 2

long spear, the favourite weapon of the phalanx-formation in many periods and areas. In the earlier part of the second millennium the spear-head had been attached to the shaft by a combination of a bent tang (sometimes with a 'button' at the end) bound into the shaft and slots in the blade through which the end of the shaft could be further lashed to the face of the blade. Similar tangs were used in attaching a metal spike to the other end of the spear. The primary function of this was to balance the weapon, but it could also be used in action to pierce an enemy, or it could be stuck into the ground during rest-periods while on the march. Later in the millennium the more efficient form of socketed spearhead was introduced. This was much less likely to come away from the shaft in action.

Plate 51

In the Anatolian hills the Hittite soldier carried the slashing-sword, a vicious-looking weapon shaped like a sickle but with the cutting-edge on the outside of the curved blade. It was not until almost the end of the second millenium that metallurgical techniques proved good enough to provide a long cutting-weapon with a straight blade. This development may have taken place in western Anatolia, if we accept that area as the

original homeland of many of the 'Peoples of the Sea' who are illustrated with long-swords on Egyptian monuments. Hittite warriors also
carried a short stabbing-sword or dagger which can often be seen on the
sculptures. This had a hilt which was frequently crescent-shaped or
(perhaps only for ceremonial use) elaborately decorated with animal
heads. Often this weapon too seems to have been slightly curved, as can
be seen both on sculptural reliefs and in actual examples from Boğazköy
and Troy. Straight blades with a wide central flange, a strengthening
device much favoured by Anatolian metalsmiths, are also to be found.
In the early part of the second millennium the handle was attached to the
blade by means of rivets, but later a more advanced form became
popular in which the blade and hilt were cast as one piece and an inlay
of wood or bone was held in position on either side of the hilt by rivets
and flanged edges. In western Anatolia there are naturally signs of
Aegean and European influences, for instance in a dagger from Thermi
with a leaf-shaped blade and a 'horned' hand-guard. The wide central
flange of this weapon, however, suggests that it is locally made rather
than an import. The eastward spread of similar influences can be seen
in the shapes of swords on reliefs at Karabel, east of Izmir, Gavurkalesi
near Ankara, and Yazilikaya, and by the early part of the first millennium they had penetrated as far south-east as Sinjerli. Many swords and
daggers had pommels of stone, bone or metal, and often these have
survived when the weapons themselves have disappeared.

Another weapon carried by the Hittite soldier was the axe. This took
two main forms, one with a hole into which the shaft was fixed and the
other a flat blade which was inserted into a split shaft and bound in
position. The earliest shaft-hole axes in Anatolia are clearly linked to
similar weapons in stone, but characteristically metal shapes were soon
evolved. Signs of influence from widely separated areas in Anatolian
examples serve to emphasize the highly international nature of metal
working in the second millennium, with smiths operating along trade-
routes which were little affected by national frontiers. Axes found at
Kültepe and dated to the earlier part of the millennium show a characteristically Assyrian raising of the blade above the level of the socket,
and may well be linked to the presence of Assyrian trading-colonies at
that site, but ribbing round the shaft-hole is a feature not only in eastern
Anatolia but also in Syria, Iran and the northern Caucasus area, and

Plate 62

Plate 62

cannot be directly linked with any particular element in the population. Perhaps the most famous Anatolian shaft-axe is that carried by the figure on the King's Gate at Boğazköy. In this sculpture the spikes at the rear of the shaft are really a development of the ribbing mentioned above, as can be seen in a Palestinian example of the fourteenth century from Beth-shan. The blade, however, is of a type which can be paralleled only in the Caucasus region. A curved wooden shaft and a tassel complete a weapon of which no archaeological example has yet been found.

Plate 24

The subject of flat axes without a socket is complicated by the fact that many examples may have been wood- or metalworking tools rather than weapons. However, it is clear that some at least were axes rather than broad chisels or adzes, and no doubt many were used in both peace and war. Such axes normally had projections or lugs on either side of the blade where it was fitted into the shaft, and were widely used in many parts of Anatolia.

The bow was also used by Anatolian armies. Sometimes it was carried on the Egyptian pattern by chariot-troops, and it was probably the weapon of the Hittite light infantry, as well as that of the Gasga and other powers. The bow itself was of the composite type, constructed of a combination of wood and horn glued and bound to form an integrated body of great strength and power. This weapon may have been introduced to Anatolia from Mesopotamia in the Akkadian period, and it can be recognized in sculptures by its characteristic shape, which shows

Plate 4

either ends that curve outwards or a triangular form with the bowstring forming its base. Arrowheads were of bronze, attached by a tang to a body made of wood or reed, and in a great many cases with barbs at the rear corners. The quiver was of leather or bark, and probably held twenty to thirty arrows.

For personal defence Hittite soldiers wore helmets, and some at least carried shields. The best representation of a helmet is that worn by the figure on the King's Gate. It has a pointed top, flaps to cover the cheeks and neck, and a long plume which hangs down the warrior's back. Hittite shields can be seen in the Egyptian representations of the Battle of Qadesh. They were made of leather on a wooden frame roughly shaped like a figure-of-eight, and were presumably designed (despite their size on the Egyptian reliefs) for whole-body protection. The remarkable

Plate 62

lack of shields among the infantry in these pictures serves to strengthen the assumption that the long garment of the Hittite troops was a coat of mail rather than 'tropical kit' or a sort of great-coat to be left with the baggage-train when swift action was intended. As shown on Anatolian monuments warriors wear a short belted tunic or a kilt that leaves the chest bare. The King's Gate figure seems to be wearing the latter garment, but it has been suggested that the markings taken by most people to represent the hair on his chest are, in fact, intended to convey the idea of a mail shirt. Towards the end of the millennium round shields were introduced by the Sea Peoples, and they became part of the normal equipment of Neo-Hittite military units.

The art of fortification is an ancient one in Antolia. The Neolithic settlement of Çatal Hüyük was defended about 6000 BC by the simple expedient (perhaps originally an architectural necessity or a defence against flood-water rather than human enemies) of building the houses without spaces between them and making all entries through the roofs. Thus any attacker was met by a solid blank wall, which was presumably high and strong enough to make his weapons ineffective. As time passed and weapons improved something stronger became necessary. The settlement of Hacılar II (*c.* 5400) has an independent wall of mud brick between 5 feet and 10 feet thick and provided with small towers which enabled the defenders to fire along the face of the wall. The slightly later (*c.* 5250) wall of Hacılar I is even more massive, and is built in a series of 'steps' to give a clear field for covering-fire in front of it. By about 4000 BC the fortress at Mersin (Level XVI), set on a hill-top, had developed further defensive refinements. Here the mud-brick wall stood on a high terraced foundation of stone (only the towers at Hacılar had stone foundations) and the sloping face of the mound below the foundations was protected by stone slabs which made access to the wall extremely difficult. The wall itself was built in a succession of straight sections with shallow offsets where it changed direction and periodic towers for lateral fire-power. Third-millennium defences show further improvements of the same basic techniques. In the north-west especially the development of architecture in stone led to a high standard of wall-construction, and the defences of Troy and Poliochni provide fine examples of sloping rubble walls crowned by a mud-brick super-structure and protected by towers and solid bastions.

Fig. 3

Fig. 4

Fig. 5

If we turn now to the defensive walls of the second millenium we can see that Anatolian architects of this period had to a great extent mastered the problems of this type of construction. It is important to remember that the purpose of a defensive structure is not merely the negative one of stopping the enemy. As well as giving security it has to restore to the defenders their superiority in mobility and fire-power. This is done by placing the defenders not merely beyond the reach of the enemy but also above them and to their sides. A wall must not merely keep the enemy out, for this would lead to a siege in which the defenders were inevitably at a disadvantage, but should be designed in such a way as to provide the defenders with an answer to whatever the enemy may try to do. Thus, although the impression one gains from the remains of defensive walls is one of enormous thickness, the principal requirement was height, setting the defenders above and out of reach of the attackers. The thickness of the wall gave height with stability and enabled the defenders to protect the weak points of the wall, the top, the bottom, the corners and the entrances. The top of the wall had to allow the defenders to move freely and to shoot without hindrance. Hence the need for battlements and for a wide roadway along the wall behind them. The bottom had to be protected from battering-rams and the area in front of it kept clear of attackers with scaling-ladders. Hence the development of the sloping lower face or glacis, which had the additional advantage of causing stones dropped from above to bounce off at unexpected angles, thus creating the maximum of havoc and confusion in the enemy ranks. The corners of the wall were in special danger of being undermined, and Anatolian builders often approached the ideal of having no corners at all. Certainly their fortifications tended to be circular rather than rectangular, and those angles which did exist were normally covered by protective towers. The same was true of gateways, the weakest point of any fortifications. An alternative design of gateway provided for one or more right-angled bends to restrict and confuse the enemy and increase the number of directions from which defensive fire could be directed.

The most important sites that serve to illustrate these principles are

Fig. 52
Plate 25

Boğazköy and Troy, but additional information from sites like Alaca, Alişar, Beycesultan, Kusura and Mersin, as well as Anatolian-influenced towns such as Alalah and Ugarit in north Syria, enables us to

Fig. 48 Plan of Boğazköy (after Bittel)

Fig. 48

Fig. 49

Plate 26

Plate 27

build up a clear picture of second-millennium defensive architecture in Anatolia. The walls of Boğazköy in the late Imperial period form a vast circuit over three miles long. They enclose an area which rises up from the older city in the north to a high rocky crest in the south, and just before the fall of the empire were even extended to include the steep hill known as Büyükkaya by twice bridging the deep gorge to the north of the citadel. The rough ground on which the wall was built was first raised to a constant level by heaping up a rampart of earth, sometimes 80 yards wide at its foot and narrowing as it rose to provide a sloping glacis which was in places faced with dressed stone. On this rampart stood the main city-wall, a 'double-casemate' construction consisting of outer and inner skins of irregular but carefully jointed masonry connected by cross-walls and having the spaces between filled with rubble. On top of this structure, some 30 feet above the earth rampart, was a further wall of mud-brick, presumably crowned by battlements such as can be seen on a fragment of an ornamental vase found in the city. Rectangular towers projected from the wall at intervals of about 100 feet, and in some places there was an additional apron-wall built some 25 feet in front of the main wall and strengthened by bastions situated midway between its towers. The main gateways were flanked by large towers to which were joined the ends of both the main wall and the apron-wall. Between these towers the bronze-covered gates were set back some distance from the front faces of the towers, and secondary gates were fitted flush with their inner faces. The gates were reached by means of steep ramps parallel to the city-wall, which would force attackers to turn their flank to the defending forces. In one case at least a

Fig. 49 Wall carried on bridge across gorge at Boğazköy (after Bittel)

0   10
      m

Fig. 50 Plan of the King's Gate, Boğazköy (after Bittel)

wall and subsidiary tower on the outer side of the ramp provided additional protection.

Fig. 50

At the southernmost point of the city was a small gate (the 'Sphinx Gate') for pedestrian use. Here the rampart was about 35 feet high, and access to the gate from outside was by means of two staircases cut into the face of the rampart some distance on either side of it. Beneath the gate, and constructed before the rampart was built, was a corbelled tunnel almost 90 yards long leading to the interior of the city. This was certainly intended to be more than a short-cut for lazy citizens. It was, in fact, a regular feature of Hittite defensive architecture, for there are further examples in what had been the south wall of the older city, as well as at Alaca, Alişar and as far afield as Ugarit. Such tunnels may well have been used for counter-attacks, either to take the enemy by surprise or to engage him when he was on the point of collapse, but the positioning of all the Boğazköy examples beneath the southern wall, on the side furthest from the constant menace of Gasgan attack, suggests that their ultimate purpose was to facilitate escape to the more friendly south of the city when on the point of capture.

Fig. 51

The outer ring-wall of Boğazköy was not its sole means of defence. Inside, the city was divided into areas which could be separately

Fig. 51 Section of wall and postern-tunnel, Boğazköy (after Akurgal)

defended if any section of the main wall fell to the enemy. The strongest of
these areas was undoubtedly the citadel, the site of the royal palace and
Fig. 32   archives, set high above the oldest part of the town. The natural security
of this site was supplemented by walls of the same type as the main city-
wall. Other walls divided the rest of the city into smaller units, some of
Fig. 27   which contained fortified buildings or secondary citadels. It is easy to
see how difficult it must have been to gain complete control of the city.

Other central Anatolian sites share many of the features of the defensive architecture of Boğazköy. At Alişar and Karahüyük near Konya,
walls dating from the Colony period and built on the casemate principle
show that this building method was by no means a Late Bronze Age
Fig. 52   invention. The town-wall of Alişar has no defensive towers; instead it is
built in a series of 'steps' rather like the much earlier Hacılar fortress.
Fig. 3   Alaca too has a ring-wall (with towers) and a typically Hittite gateway,
Plate 65   and although it lies south of the main Gasga border-line it may be taken

Fig. 52 Part of the city wall at Alişar
(after von der Osten)

as typical of a fortified border-town. A large building inside the town is usually identified as a palace and has been described in that context, but it could conceivably be a barracks for the local garrison.

The spread of Hittite influence to Cilicia at the time of the Old Kingdom can be seen at Mersin where a similar method of wall-construction was employed, with projecting towers to strengthen points where the wall changed direction. As at Alişar a street running along the inside of the wall aided rapid movement of troops in emergencies.

In western Anatolia the main features of defensive architecture are to be seen in the walls of Troy VI. These have been described at length in another volume of this series, and a few details must suffice here. Built in several sections, the wall consisted of a mud-brick superstructure built on a high stone rampart of well-worked masonry with a pronounced batter on its outer face. Changes of direction were marked by shallow offsets or steps a few inches deep. These were quite independent of the jointing of the masonry, and while this technique may have been evolved to counteract the difficulty of building sloping walls along irregular ground, it results in a complete absence of corners where the masonry is weak and undermining can be usefully attempted. Towers were thus not needed to protect the angles, and their main use was for the guarding of gates, of which the principal one (the South Gate) was a passage about 11 feet wide with a tower on one side only. The other gates were constructed to a different plan which can be best illustrated by the East Gate. Here two sections of wall overlapped to leave a passage about 6 feet wide and 16 feet long. At the inner end was a sharp bend where a

Fig. 53

Plate 28

Plate 29

Fig. 53 Plan of Troy VI (after Blegen)

0   60
⌞_____⌟ m

door was situated. Projecting from the wall face some 30 yards south of the passage was a strong rectangular tower. Thus enemy troops seeking entrance would be overlooked from both sides of the narrow passage, their movement would be impeded by the bend, and no force of any size could be gathered outside without exposing its rear to fire from the tower.

No system of fortifications, however well contrived, can be successful unless its defenders can maintain themselves for long periods without contact with the outside world. This means that there must be an ample supply of food and water inside the fortifications. Storage of food is relatively easy. Perhaps the best-known example is that of Troy VIIa with its large number of storage-jars sunk into the floor of almost every house. But a supply of water is a very different matter. Natural sources have to be protected, and if they do not exist, storage-tanks have to be provided. The principal source of water for Troy VI, for instance, was a well or cistern situated at the north-eastern corner of the citadel, formed by driving a shaft almost 14 feet square and over 30 feet deep into the natural rock. For protection this vital source was enclosed in an enormous tower built of squared limestone blocks which rose to a height of about 30 feet and supported a high superstructure of mud-brick. From this tower a stone stairway led up to the interior of the citadel to provide the inhabitants with easy access to the water. Another flight of steps led to a short passage with a pivoted door on the outside of the fortress wall. This passage was narrow and easily defensible, and was presumably used as a short cut in time of peace by those who needed water for their fields and herds.

With so handy a source, and two other wells close by, the compara-tively small citadel of Troy was amply provided with water. But a city the size of Boğazköy presented a much greater problem. An area such as this, with its lower end at least heavily inhabited, must have been able to draw on a large number of springs, streams or wells, a good many of which have been identified. On the citadel, and in the area known as Sarikale, cisterns about 6 feet across and 9 feet deep have been found cut into the rock. These doubtless served to hold water in times of emergency, but they were scarcely adequate for a long siege. A much later ('Late Phrygian') well just outside the citadel has recently been excavated. It is reached by a winding staircase of 36 steps enclosed between ashlar

Plate 30

walls about 6 feet high and protected by sentry-posts at the top and a tower at the foot. It cannot, however, have been in use in the Hittite period, for it was dug exactly where a Hittite gate had stood. The problem of water-supply in the Hittite capital has yet to be fully solved.

Finally, it should be pointed out that in seeking to defend themselves the inhabitants of second-millennium Anatolia did not put their trust solely in stone and mud-brick. No city, however strong, could stand without the protective aid of supernatural powers. At Boğazköy the King's Gate, the Lion Gate and the Sphinx Gate all have their carved portal-figures designed to keep evil influences and evil men at bay. The sphinxes on the main gate at Alaca perform the same function. At Troy the sculptural technique is poorer, but the apotropaic power is doubtless equally effective. Here outside the South Gate rectangular pillars, probably originally six in number,[33] were set up along the face of the gate-tower. These pillars have unfortunately been broken off, and so it is not clear whether their upper parts were carved or not, but their purpose seems clear. Without doubt they are to be linked with the raised altar inside the gate-tower, and with a long narrow building on the opposite side of the gate in which throughout the life of the sixth settlement burnt sacrifices were offered to the divine powers whose symbols or images stood just across the road. A similar pillar was erected outside the western gate of the citadel. But although these monoliths, aided by the stout walls, were able to deal with any human attacks, they could not cope with the superior power of the earthquake which devastated Troy VI and toppled large sections of its masonry to the ground.

Plates 62–5

Plate 31

CHAPTER VI
Society and Administration

Although our evidence for Anatolian social and political structure comes mainly from the archives of a city-dwelling upper class, it is important to remember that the basic unit of Anatolian society has long been – and to a large extent still is – the village. Hittite texts offer hundreds of place-names preceded by the determinative usually translated 'town' or 'city', but it is clear that this determinative was applied to any collec- tion of houses, however small, and that most of the towns were in fact only villages. Archaeological surveys have shown that towns of any size were comparatively few in number, and a city on the scale of Hattusas was wholly exceptional. The society in which the vast majority of the inhabitants of second-millennium Anatolia lived was not an urban one. Life was centred on the small agricultural communi- ties in which people were born, communities which were self-contained, self-sufficient, and in their essentials unaltering from year to year and down the centuries. It is easy to see that despite the many changes of government which have taken place in the intervening period the Anatolian village today is much like its predecessor over three thousand years ago. So in many cases where information is scanty or non-existent a study of modern village life[34] can lead to a fuller understanding of the life and organization of a small Hittite community.

Every village had its own cultivable territory, separated from that of neighbouring villages by uncultivated 'no-man's-land'. On its territory each village grew its crops and fed its animals, and within that territory it was responsible for the maintenance of law and order and the protec- tion of strangers. Much of the village land was held in common, but some at least could be leased to individual villagers ('men of the tool' in the Hittite Law Code) in return presumably for their services to the community as craftsmen. These land-holders had also to devote some time to labour on public works such as wells and irrigation channels.

The most important figures in village life were the Elders, who formed a governing body and were probably the senior heads of households in the community. These households were patrilineal in structure, and in them the father exercised a great deal of authority. He not only 'gave' his daughters to their prospective husbands but could even give a son to another household whose son he had killed. Wives, however, were not regarded as mere possessions of their husbands, but seem to have retained some vestiges of a more independent position. A woman of free birth, for instance, who married a slave, kept her status as a free woman. Wives had at least some say in the disposal of their daughters in marriage, and in certain circumstances (admittedly very obscure) they could disown their sons and even divorce their husbands. Although the normal marriage-arrangement was that a man 'took' a wife and 'made a house and children' with her (the phraseology suggests nuclear rather than extended families as social units, and this is not incompatible with the archaeological evidence) it was possible in some cases for a woman to remain in her father's house after marriage. On the other hand the custom of levirate marriage, by which a widow was married to her late husband's brother, father or other surviving male relative, can only have been acceptable in a society where male primacy was a recognized feature.

Mention has just been made of slaves, and there is no doubt that slavery did exist in Hittite society. Yet it is well-nigh impossible to say what proportion of the community consisted of slaves, or what part, if any, they played in the village economy. In the Imperial period at least slaves were the property of their masters, who had the power of life and death over them, but in the Old Kingdom, as reflected in the Law Code, slaves had legal rights and were able to own property. It seems likely that they were employed mainly as servants to the rich. Much more important in a village context were the large numbers of people deported from conquered countries and settled on land in Hittite territory. These deportees were not assigned to individual owners, but remained under the control of the state. The extra man-power they provided was increasingly needed in the Imperial period as increased productivity was demanded at the same time as Hittite citizens were more and more required for military duties.

Another way in which the state imposed its authority on village life can perhaps be seen in those sections of the Law Code in which prices are fixed for a large number of commodities and wages regulated

for many services. Unfortunately we do not possess the private documents which would enable us to see what effect, if any, the edicts of the
Hittite Prices and Incomes Board had on everyday life. We also lack
evidence for the possible effects of inflation on a system of fixed prices.
On the whole it is difficult to believe that the ordinary day-to-day
transactions of village life could have been rigorously controlled by
government policy.

What was the nature of the government which was superimposed on
the village system, and was in many ways alien to it? In the period preceding the rise of Hattusas Anatolia had consisted of a large number of
'city-states', each with its own fairly limited territory and its own central
palace organization, and the rise of Hattusas did not lead to any fundamental changes, but was rather an extension and elaboration of what was
by then a traditional Anatolian system. All effective power was in the
hands of a limited number of families or clans who formed an aristocracy. Among these the most important was the 'Great Family' which
provided the king and the highest officers of state, whose main function
was, if one can judge by their titles, to supervise the various departments
of the royal household. The other members of the aristocracy combined
their role as warriors with administrative duties in the palace departments, and were collectively known as the 'fighting men and servants
of the king'. As a body they also formed the *pankus* or 'whole body of
citizens'. This functioned primarily as a law-court, and members were
entitled to trial by their peers. Even the king was liable to be brought
before it, although there is no evidence that this ever actually happened.
It was moreover summoned by Hattusilis I to hear his proclamation of
his successor, if not in fact to approve or veto his choice. This has
suggested to many that the *pankus* was a relic of an Indo-European
institution, to be compared for instance with the Teutonic *teuta*,[35] and
that the position of king was, as in other Indo-European societies,
originally an elective one. But it has to be stressed that if this is so most
traces of it had disappeared long before the period of our earliest evidence,
for the *pankus* under Hattusilis I and Telepinus was an almost completely
powerless body. There is nothing to indicate that Hattusilis required its
approval for his choice of successor, and on the only occasion on which
we hear of it functioning as a court its decision was arbitrarily overruled
by the king.

Closely connected with the position of king was that of queen, and here there are many features which suggest that this lady did not hold her title merely because she was the king's consort. She retained her position after the death of her husband, and often took part in the governing of the country. This has been seen as a relic of original Anatolian matriarchy, later joined by marriage to an Indo-European system of kingship, but there is no real evidence for this.[36] More probably the queen held her position primarily because of her religious duties, and it is possible that she owed her importance originally to a system of brother-sister marriage within a closed royal family. But again if this is true it must have ceased to be the case long before the emergence of the Hittite kingdom.

Members of the aristocracy were bound by oaths of loyalty to the king, and in return for their services were given grants of land. Thus the elements of a 'feudal' system were present from the earliest days, although the word would be shunned by students of medieval western Europe, who can see no trace of the elaborate pyramid of obligations which is characteristic of genuine feudalism. The control of conquered territory was given at first to members of the royal family, and then with the extension of Hittite authority increasingly to governors and military commanders drawn from the other aristocratic families. These officials were expected to work with the Elders of their districts and to supervise the administration of justice, the due performance of festivals and the general welfare of the people, but many of them were doubtless more concerned with furthering their personal interests. In the Old Kingdom period these 'barons' were a constant threat to royal authority, especially when a king died and his successor had yet to establish himself firmly on the throne, and it was only under Telepinus that their power was defined and curtailed, and a regular rule of royal succession established.

The years between 1500 and 1400 saw vast changes in the organization of the state and the position of the Hittite king. By the Imperial period the monarch was a remote and absolute figure, the *pankus* had been abolished, and the 'feudal' organization had become much stronger. The reasons for these changes are still rather obscure. Some of them may be connected with the introduction of the light horse-drawn chariot as a weapon of war, for this was an expensive piece of equipment, the

Fig. 46

efficient operation of which required full-time training of both horse and man. In order to cope with this there was a great enlargement of the baronial class, supported by grants of state-owned land and bound by feudal ties to the king. Other changes may be due to the spread of Mesopotamian ideas of kingship into Anatolia through increasing Hurrian influence. But in many ways the differences were not so much foreign importations as developments of the old system made necessary by the increasing complexity of the expanding empire. Thus the system of local governors, drawn from the aristocracy and bound by personal oath to the king, was extended to include vassal-rulers of conquered states, who were obliged to pay homage to the Great King, to fight in his wars, and to pay a yearly tribute. In some cases the larger conquered states were given an appearance of independence by a diplomatic fiction which classed them as protectorates rather than vassals, but foreign policy always remained in the hands of the Hittite king. Occasionally, on the Gasgan frontier for instance or in northern Syria, the oldest system of all was retained, under which royal relatives were appointed as local kings to ensure the loyalty of these vital areas.

The position of a vassal was carefully defined by an elaborate treaty, introduced by a historical preamble which detailed the graciousness of earlier Hittite kings towards the vassal's ancestors, and rounded off by a long list of the gods whose wrath would descend on anyone foolish enough to break the contract. Similarly elaborate treaties were made with the other Great Powers of the day, based on the equality and 'brotherhood' of the participants, and guaranteeing such matters as united action against common enemies and the succession, on the death of either party, of his legitimate heir. Inter-dynastic marriages were a common political device, and Hittite princesses were frequently sent off to a future of doubtful marital bliss in order to cement an alliance or ensure a vassal's loyalty. Behind all this lay an international Civil Service system by means of which the powers kept in touch with each other, and through which mutually acceptable arrangements could be made. Exchanges of gifts were common, and monarchs kept up a regular correspondence with their 'brothers', as well as with the subordinate rulers of vassal states.

Although what has been said in this chapter applies primarily to the Hittites and to those parts of Anatolia which were controlled by them, there is little doubt that much of it is equally true of other areas. Village life in the west, for instance, cannot have been different in essentials from that in central Anatolia, and there is nothing to suggest that Arzawa was not controlled by a ruling family and palace organization basically similar to that of Hatti. The relationship between Arzawa proper and the other Arzawa lands is not at all clear. It may have been one of vassaldom, and it can be seen that the royal families of the lesser states were closely linked to Arzawa by a series of dynastic marriages. In the international field Arzawa suffered from being rather on the periphery of the Middle Eastern world, but the king of Arzawa was eager to have himself admitted to the brotherhood of Great Kings. Unfortunately in his case his civil service was unable to cope with Akkadian, the international language of the day, and when he wrote to his 'brother' in Egypt the correspondence had to be conducted in Hittite, the lesser language of internal Anatolian diplomacy. Doubtless this defect would soon have been remedied had the king succeeded in establishing himself as an international figure.

Little can be said of the social and political organization of the far north-west except that the site of Troy looks very much like the residence of a feudal lord and his barons, and that therefore the basic patterns detailed above may also be applied to this area. Elsewhere, in Azzi-Hayasa for instance, what little evidence we have suggests that the situation was not greatly different, while in the more remote parts some sort of tribal organization probably prevailed throughout the second millennium.

Fig. 53

CHAPTER VII
Religion

The religious beliefs and practices of a community can seldom be tidily arranged as a unified system. Often the patterns of action and belief have built up over centuries – even over millennia – with alterations and additions as outside influences enter or social and economic conditions change, until the result seems to the outsider a self-contradictory hotch-potch of meaningless ritual and largely identical deities. Hittite religion is a good example of this confusion. Its roots reach back to the Neolithic period, and numerous additions and alterations between the sixth millennium and the second result in a complicated amalgam which the Hittite theologians themselves had great difficulty in organizing into an 'official' cult and pantheon. Behind this state organization it is easy to see many of the diverse elements, native and imported, which were partially fused to form the Imperial system.

The oldest religion of Anatolia, like that of many other parts of the world, was concerned with the relationship of mankind to the great powers of nature. Of these the most important was undoubtedly the life-giving earth, the mother of all things. A lesser position was held by her consort, a deity connected with the fertilizing power of water, without whose help the earth-mother could not conceive. These powers, and many others, were essential for the well-being and continuity of life, and it was necessary both for the individual and for the community to gain and keep their favour by the regular performance of appropriate ritual actions. So each village had its own protective deities, cult-centre, mythology and festival calendar linked mainly to the agricultural year. In each village too there were witches or medicine-men, who would enact rituals to counter specific disasters or achieve specific aims.

This simple (and it must be admitted hypothetical) picture became complicated as soon as political unity began to be established on a larger scale than that of the agricultural village. When communities combined, there is little sign that one group of deities replaced another, or that

Fig. 54

Fig. 54 'Mother-goddess' figure from Çatal Hüyük. The head is restored (after Mellaart)

basically similar deities were recognized as one. The separate identity of local divinities was preserved, and the result was a pantheon of increasing size and complexity. Some gods and goddesses emerged as more power-ful than others, but the worship of the less powerful continued on the age-old pattern. For the most part these deities are now little more than names to us, but some of them were to become the principal figures of the Hittite pantheon.

Non-Anatolian peoples too played a part in the formation of Hittite religion. Of these peoples the most important were the Indo-European-speakers who arrived in Anatolia in the latter part of the third millen-nium, and the Hurrians whose influence can be increasingly seen during the course of the second. It is in fact surprisingly difficult to find anything Indo-European in the Imperial religious system. The newcomers may well have brought their Zeus with them, and his influence has been seen in some of the attributes of the thunder-wielding god of the mountain-tops who is the consort of the mother-goddess in the official pantheon.[37] Other Indo-European features have been inferred from the iconography of the Karum II period (*c.* 1940–1840) at Kültepe as seen on the impres-sions of cylinder-seals found there. In previous centuries, if one can judge from statues and idols, the mother-goddess had been supreme, but

Plate 19

on the seal-impressions we find a pantheon which is predominantly male, with the weather-god paramount and an important position given to Pirwa, a god whose close links with the horse have suggested to some a connection with horse-using Indo-European invaders. But if foreign gods achieved a temporary dominance during the Colony-period, it is clear that the mother-goddess fairly quickly regained her position of primacy. The Hittite weather-god, though a powerful deity, is very decidedly subordinate to the leading lady in the pantheon.

Hurrian influence in Hittite religion is far stronger and more wide-spread. It has been suggested in an earlier chapter that the dynasty of the Imperial period, beginning probably about 1450 with the accession of Tudhaliyas I, was Hurrian in origin, and by the end of the period the official pantheon was fully Hurrianized. This can be seen most clearly in the sculptures of the open-air santuary at Yazilikaya, where the

Plates 45, 46

assembled deities of the Hittite pantheon are arranged in Hurrian order and given names that are linguistically Hurrian. It must be stressed that syncretism of this type is late and untypical.

The religion of the Hittite Empire is thus the end-product of a long and complicated process. Most of the surviving evidence relates to the official state-cult, but this provides certain clues as to the religious activities of the smaller communities of the Anatolian plateau. Much of this tends to be classed as 'magic' rather than 'religion', but it is doubtful if the average Hittite would have recognized a difference. Elaborate rituals, making much use of 'sympathetic magic', were evolved for every purpose from averting impotence to persuading a reluctant deity to return to his shrine. Local priestesses, often known simply as 'old women', played a large part, and much of the action took place in the suppliant's house or in the open air. In this connection springs as sources of underground water were especially important. Traces of simple 'sacred springs' do not often

Plate 32

survive, but a rock-monument like Eflatun Pinar, marking as it does a perennial spring, may well be an elaborated version of a common type of open-air shrine. Other rock-monuments, such as that of Muwatallis at

Plate 33

Sirkeli and the much-worn goddess-figure at Sipylus, are clearly positioned above flowing water, and these too may be connected with similar beliefs. A possible spring-shrine on a less pretentious scale has recently been discovered near Ilgin, where a spring at the foot of a hill was provided with a rectangular stone basin, whose walls were inscribed

0 _____ 10 m

Fig. 55 Plans of shrines at Beycesultan III–II (after Lloyd)

with a long hieroglyphic inscription which includes the cartouche of Tudhaliyas IV.

Small buildings used for cult-purposes also undoubtedly existed, but so far we know little about them. A simple three-roomed structure in the residential part of the lower town at Hattusas is probably typical of the many small indoor shrines, manned by a single priest, which existed all over the country. Some buildings on the citadel also seem to be connected with domestic cult, and these too may eventually find parallels at other sites. Building C of the late Imperial period had five rooms grouped around a central open area, whose floor was sunk 5 feet below those of the surrounding rooms. On the floor were layers of mud and sand in which were numerous nests of shells and votive vessels, and there was an outlet for water in one corner. An earlier building (level IVb2) on the lower terrace of the citadel seems also to have had a central area with a drain and a sunken floor, on which lay a large painted vase in the form of a duck. Again a connection with water seems probable.

In western Asia Minor we are lucky enough to have at Beycesultan a number of Late Bronze Age shrines which were found in a trench which was opened in an effort to locate the city wall. These consist of

Figs. 55, 56

Fig. 56 Reconstruction of shrine at Beycesultan II (after Lloyd)

pairs of long narrow rooms, each about 30 feet by 10 feet, with entrances Plates 34, 35
at one short end and smaller rooms (labelled 'sacristies' by the excavators)
at the other. Towards the sacristy end of each shrine was a low platform
on which stood a pair of terracotta 'horns' backed by a low wall. The
horns themselves were decorated all over with a stamped ornament in the
form of concentric circles, and in one case a cooking-pot stood on a small
clay pillar to the right of the horns. The remains of a similar structure Plate 36
were found in a contemporary house in another part of the settlement,
and yet another example has been excavated at Kusura. In the latter
instances there is not much to suggest that these structures were anything
other than domestic hearths, but it is difficult to see the best-preserved
horns from Beycesultan as mere 'pot-holders', and the quantity of
pottery, bead necklaces and bronze implements and weapons preserved
in the rooms does not suggest ordinary domestic occupation.

If we turn now to the more imposing religious structures of Boğazköy,
we are immediately brought face to face with some of the most impressive
monuments of Hittite imperialism. With the rise of Hittite power deities
who had originally been the protectors of small agricultural communities fairly quickly found themselves the guardians of a royal house
and an extensive empire. But their basic nature, and their relation to man,
did not change. In Hittite eyes the gods were the masters, and the purpose
of man was to serve god as a good servant does his master. In return the
god, like a good master, provided protection from sickness, famine and
enemy action, and punished any bad servant who had neglected his
ritual duty. So in effect, as Hittite power grew, an ever-increasing burden
was placed on the shoulders of the king. As the gods' principal servant
he was responsible for tending all the deities of his realms, and thus
became a key figure in binding the empire into a single unified structure.
His primary duty was that of ensuring the favour of the gods by an
annual round of visits to their shrines at the seasons appropriate to their
festivals, and by what at times seems an obsessive concern with the purity
of his own person and actions. If he failed in any way to perform his
duties, the gods were angry, and it was his responsibility to find the cause
of their anger, to make amends, and to request forgiveness. In such a
situation it was difficult to discover what precise offence had been
committed, for although the gods were conceived in human terms they
did not make themselves immediately manifest to a worshipper in bodily

form in order to tell him the nature of his offence. Occasionally they would speak through the mouth of an ecstatic, more frequently they would pass on a message in a dream; but normally the nature of the offence had to be discovered by resort to divination – by examination of the entrails of sacrificial victims, by noting the flight of birds, or by means of a type of lottery of which the details remain obscure. The procedure was to ask, 'Is such⁄and⁄such the cause of god's anger?', and to go on listing possible offences until the omens gave a favourable answer. When the reason for the deity's wrath was discovered the suppliant could speak directly to his god in prayer, and it is in their prayers that we can most clearly see Hittite kings (and queens and princes) as human beings struggling with human problems and seeking answers to them. The 'plague prayers' of Mursilis II are perhaps the finest example of a Hittite monarch burdened by a sense of personal responsibility for a disaster which afflicts the state.

For the most part, however, the duties of a monarch were concerned with public ritual rather than private prayer, and the performance of his

Plate 37

duties by a Great King demanded an appropriate setting. This setting was provided by a huge temple⁄complex (Temple I) set in a prominent position in the lower city. It formed a roughly square area of some 300

Fig. 57

yards a side, surrounded by a temenos⁄wall which was partly the old wall of the lower city, but was for the most part specially built for the purpose. The temple⁄buildings themselves stood roughly in the centre of this area. The ground to the west and north⁄west (i.e. *behind* the temple from the point of view of the monarch resident in the citadel to the south⁄east) was occupied by the houses of the numerous temple personnel. These varied in size. Some were terraced down the slope of the hill along main roads with a number of smaller streets and alley⁄ways separating them into blocks. Others, especially in the northern part of the precinct, were free⁄standing, and presumably belonged to functionaries of higher rank. The approach to this residential area from the lower part of the town was by means of a monumental gateway in the middle of the north⁄western wall. On the opposite side there must have been a ceremonial entrance for the king in the immediate area of the Scribal School, a large two⁄storeyed building which stood immediately beside the temenos⁄wall to the south⁄east, alongside the only practicable route down from the citadel to the temple buildings. Between this gate and the buildings

Fig. 57 The main temple-complex at Boğazköy. A, section of old city-wall; B, temenos-wall; C, temple-buildings; D, houses; E, gate from lower city; F, open space; G, Scribal School; H, main gate (?); J, postern-tunnel

themselves the ground was completely open, offering an uninterrupted view of the temple structure. This was supported on a massive artificial terrace, about 150 yards long by 110 yards wide, which on its western side cut through earlier domestic buildings and thus represents a thirteenth-century expansion of the temple. Round the edge of this terrace were ranges of long narrow store-rooms supporting an upper storey and forming an almost totally enclosed paved area in which stood the temple itself. The principal gateway to this area was near the south-

Fig. 58

Plate 38

east corner, opposite the Scribal School, but there were three other entrances to the north-east, north-west, and south-west.

The temple-building proper was entered by an elaborate gateway designed in the characteristic Hittite manner – a central gate-room with porters' lodges to right and left, and both inside and outside this a vestibule with small rooms on either side which had large windows opening on to the outer paved area or the inner court. In a corner at the opposite end of the courtyard stood a small building used for ritual ablutions, and behind this a colonnade fronted the entrance to the innermost part of the temple, a structure built in granite rather than the limestone used for the rest of the complex. Here were situated the shrines of the deities of the temple – in this case presumably the Weather-god of Hatti and the Sun-goddess of Arinna – where the divine images stood on low platforms of stone. No cult-statue has survived, but it is known from descriptive texts that they were made largely from precious metals and must in many ways have resembled the figures carved in low relief on

Plates 45, 46

Plate 54

such monuments as Yazilikaya. Occasionally the deity would be represented by his sacred animal, as can be seen on a relief from Alaca Hüyük, or by a weapon such as a sword or spear.

It has often been pointed out that the innermost shrines of Hittite temples were not immediately accessible, or even visible, from the courtyard. Whatever went on in them was the business of a select few, and the image of the deity was kept out of sight of worshippers gathered outside. It is also worth noting that the cult-rooms, and indeed most of the rooms of the temple, received light not from the inner courtyard but from windows in the outside walls. The building was thus integrated with the outer parts of the complex rather than shut off from it.

Inside the temple area many of the great festivals of the Hittite calendar must have taken place. These consisted largely of ritual washings, sacrifices and libations in different parts of the shrine. Cult equipment included sun- and moon-discs, vessels of precious metals, and pottery

Plate 22

Plate 39

rhyta, often in the form of bulls and other animals. Not only the cult-statue, but also the royal throne and parts of the temple-building itself were regarded as sacred, and *huwasi*-stones, upright stelae set in a special carved base, also had an important part to play. 'Great Assemblies', presumably in the courtyards, were a frequent occurrence, and there were constant processions by the king and his bodyguard, priests, dignitaries,

TEMENOS WALL

Fig. 58 Plan of Temple I at Boğazköy (after Bittel)

0   25   50
m

and temple-servants, often accompanied by singers and musicians playing several types of instrument.

The temple was not merely the building in which the great festivals
took place, but also the home of the god throughout the year. In it he had
his dining-room and his bedroom, and he had at his command a host of
temple-servants to attend to his every need. Some at least of these servants
presumably occupied the houses at the rear of the temple-precinct, but
others lived in the residential part of the town and others again may have
Fig. 58   lived and worked in a curious, irregularly shaped complex about 400
feet long and 180 feet wide, situated immediately south-west of the main
temple buildings, separated from them by a 25-foot-wide paved road,
and entered by a single gateway immediately opposite one of the subsidiary temple-entrances. The gateway leads to a trapezoidal courtyard
nearly 100 feet long with a maximum width of about 50 feet. Surrounding this courtyard, and opening off it, or off alleyways or corridors
leading from it, are sixteen independent units of different sizes. The whole
complex has been compared to similar Egyptian workers' compounds at
Amarna and Deir-el-Medineh.

There are other building-complexes, beside those already mentioned,
within the area of the temple-precinct, but they are for the most part still
imperfectly known. A large rectangular building (Complex 2), com-
parable in many ways to the buildings in the citadel, lay immediately
south of the workers' compound, and behind it, in an open square, was a
Fig. 59   small subterranean pool covered by a low corbel-vault and entered from
Plates 40, 41   the north by a flight of stone steps. Water entered the pool through a hole
in the back wall, and was carried off under the steps to a channel beneath

Fig. 59 Section of subterranean pool at Boğazköy (after Bittel)

0   3
     m

the road outside. Over the entry to this grotto was an incised group of figures of which only one survives, with traces of a second. The intact figure is that of a man facing left, wearing a long robe and a round cap, and raising his arm in the conventional gesture of adoration. Everything points to a non-secular use for this structure which once again lays emphasis on the divine connections of spring-water.

Four other temples are known, all of them in the southern part of the city. Three of them may have been enclosed by a single temenos-wall, and all are skilfully sited on natural plateaux overlooking the lower town. Despite differences of detail they correspond closely in plan to Temple I. Each has a ceremonial entrance, a central courtyard with colonnade, and an offset inner sanctuary with windows opening to the outside rather than to the court. Temples II, III and IV have one cult-room each. Temple V, like Temple I, has two, but in this case, for some unknown reason, one of the two was built to one side of the courtyard rather than at the end of it.

About three-quarters of a mile north-east of Boğazköy lies Yazilikaya, the most impressive of all Hittite religious structures. Here, at a point where a spring of fresh water once flowed, is an outcrop of rock which forms two natural chambers of different sizes. The site is in many respects like other Anatolian spring-sanctuaries, and may well have been a place of worship for hundreds of years before the rise of Hittite power. The first stage in its elaboration was the building, perhaps about 1500 BC, of an irregular wall which shut off the main chamber from the outside world. Under Hattusilis III this was replaced by a temple-complex with a strong resemblance to the temples of the capital. A large gate-building contained a staircase which led through a second gate into a rectangular courtyard containing an altar and a detached lustration-room. A pillared gateway to the left then led into the principal chamber, which took the place of the inner cult-rooms of the city buildings. A second gatehouse beyond the courtyard and its subsidiary rooms at first gave access to the smaller chamber, but after a fire in the temple during the reign of Tudhaliyas IV the rooms at the back of the courtyard were rebuilt and turned towards an entrance which led from the larger into the smaller chamber; the whole complex was converted into a single unit.

The principal interest of Yazilikaya however lies not in the temple buildings but in the figures carved in low relief on the rock walls of the

Fig. 60
Plates 44–51

A

B

feet 0   25   50   75   100

Fig. 60 Plan of Yazilikaya (after Akurgal)

Fig. 61
Plates 44–6

two natural chambers. Those in the larger one (Chamber A) give the
impression of two processions, one of male and one of female deities,
advancing on either side towards the rear wall, where the principal god
and goddess, emphasized both by their positions and by their greater
size, confront one another at the focal point of the chamber. Near the
rear of the right-hand procession is the figure of a Hittite king, again on a Plate 47
larger scale, identified by his accompanying cartouche as a Tudhaliyas.
Behind him a narrow passage, guarded at its entrance by a pair of demons
with wings and lion-heads, leads to the smaller chamber (Chamber B), Plate 48
a smooth-walled cleft no more than 9 feet wide with a subsidiary
chamber, some 30 feet deep, opening off its north-eastern corner. At
the back of this subsidiary chamber a wall of cyclopean masonry shuts it
off from the outside world except at the left-hand end, where a narrow
staircase provided an entry, possibly for the priest in charge of whatever
went on in this holy-of-holies. In front of the wall is a smoothed limestone
base, and the fill around it proved on excavation to contain a great deal of
wood ash. On the wall of Chamber B, next to the entry to the subsidiary
chamber and clearly connected with it, is another Tudhaliyas cartouche,
and further down the same wall is the most arresting and tantalizing
sculpture of all. It represents an enormous sword, apparently driven into Plate 49
the rock, for the lower part of the blade is not represented. The hilt of the
sword consists of two lions hanging head downwards, surmounted by
the foreparts of two more lions facing right and left, and then by a human
head facing towards the subsidiary chamber and shown by its high
pointed hat to be that of a deity. Behind this great carving, some 11 feet
high, is a smaller group of two figures. The larger, identified as the god Plate 50
Sharruma, embraces the smaller (a Tudhaliyas again) in a protective
gesture which unites the two figures into a single composition. On the
opposite wall, and again facing towards the subsidiary chamber, is a
group of twelve soldier-like deities (who also appear at the rear of the Plate 51
male procession in the outer chamber) moving menacingly at a fast trot
with their sickle-swords at the slope across their shoulders.

The problems of interpreting the sculptures of Yazilikaya in terms of
ritual and belief have certainly not all been solved. It has been pointed
out by the excavator that the temple buildings, unlike those of the
capital, were flimsily constructed and cannot have supported an upper
storey. This suggests to him that they were not in daily use, but were

Fig. 61 The rock-reliefs in Chamber A at Yazilikaya (after Garstang)

reserved for some special function, perhaps an annual event.[38] This event, he plausibly suggests, was the great spring festival, held at the beginning of each new year, lasting over a month, attended by all the gods, and perhaps culminating in a 'sacred marriage' of the type so diligently documented by Sir James Frazer.

This interpretation, well as it fits the larger chamber, cannot be applied to the smaller, which must have had a different purpose. Any attempt to discover this purpose must take into account the private nature of this inner 'chapel' and the significance of the huge sculpture portraying the

28   34   39

49   55   63

sword in the rock. The nearest parallel to this curious weapon dates from the colony-period and is dedicated to the god of the underworld. A Hittite ritual text dealing with gods resident in the underworld describes how a priest makes images of them in the shape of swords and fixes them into the ground. Moreover, in another text the god of the underworld is connected with 'the twelve gods of the cross-roads' (whoever they may be), and one is reminded of the twelve running gods on the western wall. To all this must be added the fact that burials were found in the rocks surrounding the chamber, and that sometimes these included bird as well

Fig. 62 Figures of Tudhaliyas (left) and Sharruma (right) from Yazilikaya

Fig. 62

as human skeletons. In one case for instance a bird had been pinned down in position by fourteen large nails. Since birds are known from texts to have been sacrificed to the deities of the underworld, the excavator's conclusion that the inner chamber is a mortuary chapel of some kind is almost irrefutable.[39] The connection with Tudhaliyas (presumably the fourth of that name, since he is known to have regarded Sharruma as his protective deity) suggests that it was dedicated either to that monarch after his death or by him to some ancestor, probably an earlier namesake. A statue may well have stood at the northern end of the chamber or in the subsidiary chamber, and one of the small rectangular recesses which have been cut into the walls may have contained the ashes of the dead king.

This conclusion leads us to the subject of burial practices. Evidence for these again comes from both textual and archaeological sources. Graveyards are known from near Boğazköy, from Ilica some forty miles west of Ankara, from the later Phrygian capital Gordion, and from near Hissarlik, the reputed site of Troy. In every case they contain the graves of ordinary people. Royal tombs laden with gold, such as are to be found in contemporary kingdoms like Egypt and Mycenae, have not been discovered in Anatolia. The only possible exception to this is the structure known as Gavurkalesi, south-west of Ankara, where a terraced

Fig. 63
Plate 3

Fig. 63 Plan of Gavurkalesi (after Akurgal)

processional way leads to a hill-top plateau, some 40 yards square, fortified by walls of cyclopean masonry. At the head of the ascent a natural rock-face bears a carved relief showing two gods advancing to confront a seated goddess, while at the rear of the plateau lies a burial chamber, long since robbed, measuring about 13 feet by 10 feet. This could well be the type of grave in which we know from textual evidence that the remains of monarchs were deposited.

Hittite kings were cremated, and comparisons have often been made between their funerals and those of the heroes of the Homeric poems.[40] Since until recently no tradition of cremation was known to exist in either the Mycenaean or the Hittite world, and since the graveyard at Troy, dated to the latest phase of Troy VI, consists entirely of cremation burials, the argument was that both the Homeric and the Hittite rituals were adopted through contact with north-west Anatolia. More recent evidence suggests that this is an over-simplification. Cremation is now known to have been practised in Greece as early as the Middle Bronze Age,[41] and to have been widespread in central Anatolia from the very beginning of the Hittite period. The excavation of a large number of cremation-graves at Gedikli, in the plain of Islâhiye in south-eastern Turkey, which are clearly dated to the E.B. III period (i.e. the latter part of the third millennium) gives a pointer to the direction from which the practice may have come and the presence of vessels of the type Schliemann termed *depas amphikypellon* in the Gedikli graves shows a clear connection with Troy II, although the nature of this connection is not yet fully understood. Cremation-graves in Greece, such as those in the cemetary at Perati, also point to connections with the Levantine area.

There are now many examples of cremation-burial in Late Bronze Age Anatolia, and the cemetery at Troy is only one of several known and excavated. The graves there lay on the southern edge of the plateau about 550 yards south of the citadel. The ashes of the dead were placed in jars of different shapes and sizes, which were covered with a lid and stood upright in shallow graves, often only a few centimetres below the surface of the ground. Funeral gifts were few in number and of no great intrinsic value – beads, small pottery vessels and a few pins and rings of bronze. There is no sign that graves were individually marked, or that the grave-yard had any sort of boundary-marking. A walled enclosure below the western foot of the citadel showed abundant traces of burning in associa-

Plate 42

tion with the remains of human bones, and another mud-brick structure, some 220 yards north-west of the cemetery, may have been a furnace. This is reminiscent of the earlier graveyard at Gedikli, where there were also hearths for the burning of the dead in the area where they were finally laid to rest.

The cemetery at Boğazköy also lies outside the city, beside the road which leads to the Yazilikaya shrine. Here large numbers of burials, some cremations and others simple inhumations, were tucked into niches and crevices in the natural rock. Stratigraphically the graves cover a period from the eighteenth to the fourteenth century. Again the remains were deposited in pottery vessels of different shapes and sizes, many of which, like those at Troy, were already broken when they were used as funerary urns. This may be a sign of poverty, or it may have some ritual significance. Grave-gifts were restricted to shells, small pots, some bronze wire, and one stamp-seal. Many graves are distinguished by the presence of animal remains. The bones of cattle, sheep and pigs presumably represent the remains of some sort of funeral feast; dog-bones tend to be taken as evidence for man's desire for faithful companionship in the other world, but there is textual evidence for dog-sacrifice with magical or ritual associations. The remains of horses (two skulls and a number of fragments) may be significant in showing some sort of ultimate connection with the practice of the nomadic pastoralists of the Russian steppe, and thus providing a tenuous link with the *Kurgan*-peoples who are thought to have introduced Indo-European languages to Anatolia. The presence of eleven donkey-skulls and other bone-fragments suggests that some inhabitants of Hattusas could not afford a sacrificial horse and had to make do with a cheaper alternative.

One disturbing feature of the cemetery was that a high proportion of the burials which survived intact contained the remains of an adult and a child buried together. This may be nothing more than coincidence, but the possibility of some sort of child-sacrifice cannot be excluded.

The graveyard at Ilica, which can be dated to the Old Hittite period, also consists of mixed cremations and inhumations, but with the former predominating. Here the remains were deposited in damaged beak-spouted vessels and buried with the spouts facing east. Again there are animal bones, and grave-gifts are few. What distinguished this site is the presence of megalithic grave-markers, or rather row-markers, s

for they do not serve to distinguish individual graves. These are arranged to form one or two lines about 220 yards long. Originally there may have been far more of them, and in fact markers may have been typical of many contemporary cemeteries, though in most cases they have long ago been removed.

Ilica lies only about 40 miles from Gordion, so it is surprising to find that the cemetery at that site, which is in part contemporary with Ilica, contains no known cremation-burials at all, but consists entirely of inhumations, some in simple earth-graves, some in cist-graves, but the great majority in *pithoi*. It is probable that the simple inhumations were the earliest (dated to the colony-period), and that by the Old Hittite period most if not all the burials were in *pithos*-graves. Skeletons in the *pithoi* were buried in a contracted position with the head towards the south-east. The lack of cremations may represent a genuine difference in local burial-habits, but more probably it means that cremation-graves exist at Gordion but have yet to be found.

Gedikli, the site which has yielded third-millennium cremations, has also provided some simple inhumations dated perhaps to the middle of the second millennium, and recently the Ankara Museum has acquired pottery from Ferzant, near Merzifon, which suggests the existence of another Old Hittite cemetery.

Despite the use of extra-mural cemeteries, it is clear that intra-mural inhumation was also fairly common. At Boğazköy, for instance, bodies were often buried in or near the houses. Most were placed in simple earth-graves, but there were departures from this – burial under stone slabs, and in one case disposal under the two halves of a *pithos* cut length-wise. Grave-gifts in intra-mural burials were also few in number and poor in quality. All burials in and round the city seem to be those of ordinary citizens, and no social distinctions can be made in terms of type or location of burial.

Plate 43

CHAPTER VIII

Art and Literature

The immediate reaction of anyone who turns to the art of Anatolia between 1650 and 1200 BC and compares it with the art of neighbouring lands is one of disappointment. This is the period which in Egypt pro-duced the tomb-paintings of the earlier New Kingdom, the sensitive naturalism of the Amarna period, the opulence of the tomb of Tutan-khamun, and the technical brilliance of the great battle-scenes of the Nineteenth Dynasty, while in the Aegean world the fresco-painting of the Minoan and Mycenaean palaces, the seal-stones of Crete and the metalwork of the Shaft Graves have a notable place in any history of world art. In comparison with these Anatolia has almost nothing to offer. There is little imagination, delicacy, creative flair or technical accomplishment in its art, only a crude vigour which is the immediately recognizable hall-mark of both large- and small-scale works. This may be partially due to the accidents of survival – there are no sumptuously appointed royal tombs, for instance, to provide 'treasures' which in other circumstances have perished – but there is no doubt that in places such as the palace and temples at Boğazköy where one might have expected some sign of artistic talent there is virtually no indication that it was ever on display. It has indeed been suggested that the decoration on Hittite relief vessels copied painted stucco reliefs on the walls of Hittite build-ings, and that these in turn were inspired by Syro-Mesopotamian frescoes such as those at Mari and Alalah; but although fragments of painted wall-plaster have been found at Hittite sites there is at present no evidence for any pictorial wall-decoration of any kind.[42] Small-scale works of art are remarkably few in number, and those which have survived betray no great inspiration. Even low-relief carving on natural rock, almost the only type of art which can be recognized as an original Hittite contribution, only occasionally rises above mediocrity. It is not surprising that the Hittites have been dubbed a people of 'sluggish emotions', 'intellectually unpretentious' and 'devoid of the finer graces'.[43]

Plate 21

139

Certainly if their political supremacy was accompanied by any surge of artistic talent it must have been expressed in ways which have left no trace or which we fail to recognize today.

These words may be considered by some to be too condemnatory, but there is little doubt that the average quality of Hittite work was low. Yet this is not to deny that there are one or two examples of very high quality, or that there is some point in looking at the products of Hittite artists with a view to analyzing their aims and techniques. For this purpose the rock-sculptures provide a sufficiently large corpus of material to enable us to draw some general conclusions. They are for the most part carved on

Plates 34, 45–51, 60, 61

exposed faces of natural rock, which are cut back to form a smooth back-ground from which the figures stand out in relief. In some cases the natural rock is replaced by Cyclopean stonework in an architectural

Plates 27, 52–9, 62–5

setting, as for instance on the sides of city gates, but in such situations the rock on which the carving is made is normally an essential part of the wall rather than a decorative slab applied externally to it. The result in both cases is that the sculpture becomes an integral part of its setting, and that the setting as a whole is an essential part of the work and gives it a power and vitality which can be felt *in situ* but which is almost entirely lost when the work is seen out of context (and this applies to the illustra-tions to this book). Sometimes the artist has emphasized this unity of sculpture and setting by making the sculpture in a very real sense emerge from, rather than superimposing it on, the rock. Thus the gate-lions

Plate 64

at Boğazköy have a convincing corporeality when seen in front view, but no attempt has been made to portray a side view visible as one passes through the gate. The same is true of the guardian sphinxes at

Plate 65

Alaca, where the sides of the blocks have been used for entirely different figures. But perhaps the finest example of the technique is the 'sword-god'

Plate 55

in Chamber B at Yazilikaya. The symbolic meaning of this may not be entirely clear, but its effect on the viewer is immediate and powerful.

Some Hittite sculptures however show a different technique. The

Plate 63

gate-sphinxes from Boğazköy, unlike those at Alaca, are carved to provide a side view as well as a frontal one, and the same is true of the

Plates 52, 53

splendid figure of a lion seizing a calf, also from Alaca.

Sculptures are normally in low relief, but there are some exceptions.

Plate 62

The head of the figure on the King's Gate at Boğazköy, for instance, shows almost three-quarters of the face standing out from the stone, and the unused (and probably unfinished) figure abandoned on a hillside at Fassilar protrudes so far as to be almost a sculpture in the round. Within the low reliefs there are two very different techniques. Some sculptures are almost flat, with what little detail there is shown by engraved lines. In some cases they are so lacking in any kind of modelling that they have been suspected of being unfinished. In other sculptures (mainly in or near the capital) the relief is much more rounded and plastic, with a great deal of attention paid to the treatment of muscles, details of clothing and so on. Foreign influence, possibly Hurrian or Babylonian, has been suspected as the cause of this, but there is little contemporary Mesopotamian relief with which to compare the Hittite examples, and it is equally possible that the technique was a development of a local school.

Plates 60, 61

Hittite art is basically naturalistic, in the superficial sense that it portrays human beings, animals and occasionally objects. But this certainly does not mean that there is any attempt at portraiture, or at the portrayal of individual natural scenes. The art is rather 'idealistic' and 'conceptual' in the sense that the artist's aim is not to copy accurately what he sees before him but to convey with the maximum of clarity what he considers to be the 'essence' of what he is carving. Thus in the conventional male figure the head is shown in profile whereas the shoulders and chest appear frontally; the legs and feet, however, are again in profile. These mixed figures are not the result of incompetence on the part of Hittite artists. They are in Hittite terms (and in the terms of other Middle Eastern art) ideal representations, showing what were regarded as the essential elements of 'manliness'. No attempt is made to show background or to relate the sculptures to a context other than that of the rock on which they are carved. The principal purpose is to evoke feeling rather than to portray fact.

Although many of the carvings do not in themselves have any great technical merit, the conventional position of the figures has several artistic advantages. First, it gives the impression of a steady, stately advance which adds life and movement to the sculptures. Second, and more important, it gives rise to the possibility of composition, either by the rhythmic repetition of figures to form a procession-like frieze or by the antithetical confrontation of two figures placed face to face. Both these techniques can be seen in the relief at Gavurkalesi, but by far the most elaborate example is in Chamber A at Yazilikaya. Here the feeling

Plate 3

Plate 48

Plate 51
Fig. 61
Plate 46

Fig. 62

Plate 50

Fig. 40

of two columns advancing to meet at the focal point of the chamber is overwhelming. As a rule figures do not overlap and there is no attempt at three-dimensional representation, but in some groups the slow movement of the procession is speeded up to a controlled trot by overlapping the figures and slightly altering the position of their legs. The composition of the central group is more elaborate than this, for where the deities who lead the two processions meet face to face the dramatic unity of the scene is emphasized by the addition of opposed prancing bulls which can be seen *behind* the deities' legs on either side. Thus an unusual element of depth is given to the group at the expense, it has been pointed out, of theological accuracy, for in Hittite religion the bulls are the companions of the god and have no connection with the goddess.[44]

The finest example of Hittite pictorial composition, however, is in Chamber B. Again the starting-point is the conventional position, but here the two figures, those of King Tudhaliyas IV and his personal deity Sharruma, are not merely juxtaposed but united in a way which is both emotionally powerful and artistically satisfying. In this case the figures are superposed with the god standing alongside the king, and the scale of the two is arranged so that the god, instead of holding the usual weapon in his left hand, clasps the right wrist of the king in a protective embrace. The organic coherence which this gives to the group is emphasized by the way in which the king's head fits into the curve of the god's shoulder. The whole forms a carefully organized composition, basically triangular but artistically modulated by the sweeping curves of the outline and the softly rounded modelling so that the god's extended right arm, the king's long garment and trailing *lituus*, the tilt of the high pointed hat and even the crescentic pommel of the sword are utilized and unified in a work of the very highest quality. It has to be emphasized that the idea of this grouping was not an inspiration on the part of the Yazilikaya artist. A similar arrangement of king and protective deity had appeared on seals since the time of Muwatallis; but in the rock-carving at Yazilikaya it achieved its final and finest expression.

The reliefs which have been discussed so far are concerned with religion, and are subject to hieratic conventions. Other sculptures deal with more secular subjects, and the rules which apply to them are in many ways different. This can be seen by an examination of the sculptures on either side of the Sphinx Gate at Alaca. Some of these are typically 'processional', but others show acrobats, musicians and hunting scenes. The relationship between the two types is not completely clear, but it does seem likely that both would have been seen simultaneously on the same wall. The circus figures are a fairly clumsy attempt to escape from the rules applying to religious sculptures. In some instances (e.g. the sword-swallower or the man carrying a dog) the attempt almost succeeds, but in others it is a disastrous failure. The conventional pose makes it almost impossible to play a guitar or climb a ladder convincingly. But when the sculptor turns to animals the result is a work of much higher quality. In the hunting scenes a fine freedom of vigorous naturalistic movement is achieved by a bold use of outline, and this is attractively combined with a decorative formalism of such features as horns, manes and claws. Sometimes the decorative element is even extended to include the application of palmette motifs (e.g. on the haunches of the stags) and the provision of formalized 'vegetation' as scenery. In many ways the combination is more reminiscent of steppe-art than of that which we normally consider Hittite.

A similar contrast between animal and human representation is to be seen in art products on a smaller scale. Vessels in the form of animals, notably the pair of bulls found on Büyükkale, have a lively and whimsical charm which is immediately attractive, and the rearing horse on a rein-guide found at Yozgat, though clumsy in technique, shows a similar vigour and personality in the head and the twist of the elongated neck. Statuettes of deities on the other hand tend to be much more formal and to follow in three dimensions the rules which apply to rock-relief. Of large-scale free-standing sculpture in stone practically nothing survives. The almost completely rounded figure at Fassilar and the lower part of a statue found at Alaca do not inspire great confidence in its quality, but the features of the gate-figures at Boğazköy and the fragment of a more than life-size human head found at the same site suggest that in the capital at least a much higher standard of workmanship was reached.

Outside Hittite territory there is little which can be included in a chapter on art. At Beycesultan, for instance, there is no sign that the inhabitants knew how to use a chisel, far less produce sculpture with it. Yet the impression given by this site may be misleading, for further west at Sipylus and Karabel are rock-sculptures that look typically Hittite. These have often been taken to be memorials of conquest set up by

Plate 54

Plate 55

Plate 56

Plates 57–9

Plate 22

Plate 68

Plates 66, 67

Plate 4

143

Hittite kings, but the evidence available rather suggests that they were religious in purpose and carved on the orders of local monarchs. We may indeed be mistaken in thinking of Anatolian rock-sculpture as purely Hittite in style and origin. The little that we know of Old King-dom sculpture suggests that it was in many ways different from that of the Imperial period, and it is possible that the development of the Imperial style was due to the introduction of elements from other areas, one of which may have been western Anatolia. Much more evidence is required before any final conclusions can be reached.

When we turn to the literary productions of the Hittite period it is necessary to clear our minds of possible misconceptions. Talk of 'literature' in an ancient Middle Eastern society does not imply the existence of works of creative imagination circulated to a reading public. A reading public simply did not exist. Nor can we accept that the literature we possess is what was preserved in written form at the end of a long tradition of popular oral literature. There is no evidence, for instance, that Hittite epic, though it does contain some 'formulaic' elements, is basically oral poetry 'frozen', as Homeric epic was, by the introduction of writing. On the contrary it seems clear that those elements are merely literary reminiscences of Mesopotamian technique, and that texts which we like to think of as literary were preserved only as part of the Mesopotamian system of training scribes in the art of writing. Much of this training took the form of copying texts, and in this con-nection there grew up a body of 'traditional' texts which were copied and re-copied in scribal schools all over the cuneiform world. 'Literary' texts formed a fairly small part of this collection, being far outnumbered by omen-texts, word-lists and similar documents. Why individual literary texts should have been included in the corpus is not clear, but it can be assumed that their survival is due much more to educational conservatism than to any desire to preserve works for their popularity or literary merit.

The same conservative attitude meant that there was a strong tendency towards word-for-word preservation of texts. However, the wording of many documents did vary with the passing of time, and in areas on the periphery of Mesopotamian civilization (as Hattusas was) adaptations were allowed to suit local scribal taste, translations of Mesopotamian texts into local languages were made, and at least some local material was added to the original corpus. The result is that literary texts preserved at Hattusas, although they are in many cases primarily Mesopotamian in conception, often have a 'flavour' which is recognizably Hittite. Thus the Gilgamesh epic appears in the Boğazköy archives not only in an Akkadian version, but also in translation into Hurrian and Hittite, and from what survives of the Hittite version it can be seen that those parts which dealt with the city of Uruk, and were presumably of interest mainly to a Mesopotamian audience, were shortened for Anatolian consumption, while the episode of the struggle with Huwawa, which was set in Hurrian territory far from the main centres of Mesopotamian learning, seems to have been expanded for the benefit of readers in that area, and suggests, like the translation into Hurrian, that the epic reached the Hittites through Hurrian intermediacy. Other foreign literary material is also predominantly Hurrian, although often there is evidence for Akkadian prototypes. In other instances the original is clearly Canaanite.

The best preserved texts concerned with a Hurrian milieu are those which deal with the god Kumarbi, his seizure of the kingship of the gods and his unsuccessful struggle to regain it after being replaced by Teshub. The Kumarbi compositions are of interest not only for the parallels they provide for episodes in Hesiod and other Greek authors but also because they can be seen to have a metric structure. The normal line consists basically of two cola, in each of which there are two stressed and a varying number of unstressed syllables. This metric pattern is probably not a native growth, but is, like so much else, derived from Mesopotamia. Each line contains a single syntactical clause, and this with the habitual repetition of speeches and descriptions of incidents, gives the verse a measured dignity which can be seen only in a fairly long extract. This is given here in the translation of Professor H. G. Güterbock, who has followed the original as closely as possible, even at the expense of normal English word-order.

> *Kumarbi to Impaluri began to speak :*
> *'O Impaluri! The words which I speak to thee,*
> *To my words thine ear hold inclined!*
> *Into thy hand a staff take,*
> *upon thy feet as shoes the swift winds put!*

And to the Irshirra-gods go,
and these strong words before the Irshirras speak:
"Come!
   He calls you, Kumarbi, the gods' father, to the gods' house!
But the matter about which he calls you
.   .   .   .
Now come promptly."

And the Irshirras will take him, the child,
and they will carry him to the dark earth.
But the Irshirras .   .   .   .
but not to the great gods will he be visible.'
When Impaluri the words heard,
into his hand the staff he took,
upon his feet the shoes he put.
And forth he travelled, Impaluri,
and to the Irshirras he came.

And Impaluri the words to the Irshirras again began to speak:
'Come!
   He calls you, Kumarbi, the gods' father!
But the matter about which he calls you,
that ye know not.
Now hurry, come.'
When the Irshirras the words heard,
they hurried, hastened,
and from their chair they rose.
And at once they covered the way,
and to Kumarbi they came.
And Kumarbi to the Irshirras began to speak:
'This child take,
and as a gift treat him,
and to the dark earth carry him!'

And so the action moves gradually on. The pace is slow, but repetitions are seldom exact, and this helps to keep things moving and avoid monotony.

Mythological texts of local origin do exist in the Hittite records, but it is clear that they are not works of literature in the same sense as those just discussed. Not only are they much less sophisticated both in detail and in over-all construction, but they are closely linked to cult and ritual in a way in which the foreign examples are not. The story of the Vanishing God and his return, for instance, is part of a ritual for regaining the good-will of a deity towards an individual, while the recital of the tale of the Storm-god's fight with the Dragon is part of the *purulli*-festival held at the holy city of Nerik. The texts are of the greatest interest to students of folk-lore and religion, but apart from an element of crude vigour their literary merit is extremely small.

As well as the epic-mythological past the Mesopotamian world was deeply interested in the semi-legendary past of the early historical mon-archs. In this connection Sargon and Naram-Sin, the most powerful monarchs of the Dynasty of Akkad, were among the major figures, and an extensive literature grew up around them, some at least of which was translated into Hittite and included in the archives of Hattusas. But it is important to remember that the rulers of Akkad were remembered not merely for the greatness of their achievements but also for the disastrous ends to their reigns. In their lives Mesopotamian theologians saw a pattern of divine favour, human offence and divine retribution, which provided them with a systematic framework for the interpretation of history. This idea that the past was not a random succession of incidents but a pattern of connected events was something which the Hittites developed, again in their own characteristic way. For them, although divine favour was of supreme importance, disaster was due much less to its withdrawal than to human wickedness and mismanagement. So a native legend like that of the Siege of Urshu, which deals with the attempts of an early Hittite monarch to capture an enemy town, lays the blame for his lack of success neither on the gods nor on the king's failure to treat them correctly, but on the bungling incompetence of the generals involved and their inability to carry out their orders as instructed. In this instance there is no sign (at least in the surviving part of the story) that a moral was drawn for the benefit of contemporary generals, but from the earliest days of the Old Kingdom Hittite monarchs in their decrees can be seen explicitly making use of the past to point a moral for the present. Hattusilis I, for instance, in naming his grandson Mursilis I as his successor, orders his principal servants always to obey the royal word, for only in this way will Hattusas stand high and the land be at peace. In his grandfather's time that king's servants had disobeyed him and set a usurper on the throne. 'How many of them', asks the king rhetorically, 'escaped their fate?' Even more explicit is the opening of the Telepinus decree, where the king examines the early history of the realm and ascribes its success to the harmony which then existed in the royal family, while contemporary disasters are seen as resulting from break-up of that harmony. In thus examining the past, stressing its value and interpreting its patterns in terms of human behaviour rather than supernatural intervention, these early Hittite monarchs and their scribes have a reasonable claim to anticipate Herodotus in being described as Fathers of History.

Other Herodotean features of Hittite court scribes are their talent for vivid narrative and their ability to create living characters. Their works consist mainly of decrees, annals and treaties, but even in these contexts they seldom strike the reader as being merely formal and conventional. On the contrary there is in them a gift for language which seems unforced and spontaneous, and a feeling for dramatic tension which can paint a scene or illustrate a character in an entirely original way. Typical examples are the craggy righteousness of Hattusilis I while his sister 'bellows like an ox' before him because her son is no longer heir to the throne; or the utter incredulity of Suppiluliumas when a messenger unexpectedly offers his son the throne of Egypt – 'Such a thing has never happened to me in my whole life!' Scenes such as these give official Hittite texts a life and a personal quality which is extremely attractive, and which certainly justifies their inclusion in a chapter on literature.

Mention has been made in an earlier chapter of the prayers which are preserved in the Hittite archives. These texts too illustrate many of the points which have already been made. Their basic form and many of the concepts of them are, like so much else, borrowed from Mesopotamia, but in Hattusas they are adapted and infused with local feeling until they are transformed into something new. Although they do not show the originality of expression, the complexity of structure or the depth of religious thought which would give them any great literary stature, there is in them a genuine feeling of suffering and mental conflict, a simple, straightforward philosophy of life, and a talent for homely unforced expression which makes them typically Hittite. Life, they say, is bound up with death and death with life. Man is mortal, and man is sinful. Even if a man is himself innocent the sins of his father fall upon him, he is afflicted by sickness and misery, and the anguish of his heart is impossible to endure. But when a man cries to a god for mercy the god listens to him, for god is merciful, a sheet-anchor in time of trouble. As a bird flies to its nest for refuge and the nest saves its life, so man seeks and finds refuge in god. 'Then beam on me like the full moon', cries the sufferer, 'shine over me like the sun in the sky; walk on my right hand; join with me like a yoked pair of oxen; walk by my side as a true god should.' One is reminded of King Tudhaliyas in the embrace of his protective deity in Chamber B at Yazilikaya. But even in the midst of these figurative flights the Hittite worshipper retains his down-to-earth common sense. Divine self-interest alone, he points out to his deity, should be sufficient justification for his release from suffering. After all, in killing off those who bring him offerings the god is in the end merely damaging himself. Much more to the point would be the transfer of the sufferings to enemy territory, where a supply of suitable scapegoats is conveniently available.

All the literature that has so far been mentioned belongs, as has been said, to the world of the royal court and the scribal schools. This is not to say that there was no unofficial popular literature. Doubtless songs were sung and tales were told not only in Hattusas but throughout Anatolia. A few lines of a soldiers' song are indeed preserved in a semi-historical text of the Old Kingdom period:

> *Nesas waspas, Nesas waspas*
> *tiya-mu, tiya.*
> *nu-mu annas-mas katta arnut*
> *tiya-mu, tiya.*
> *nu-mu uwas-mas katta arnut*
> *tiya-mu, tiya.*

> *Clothes of Nesas, clothes of Nesas*
> *Put on me, put!*
> *Bring down to me those of my mother;*
> *Put on me, put!*
> *Bring down to me those of my [uncertain];*
> *Put on me, put!*

The rhythmic structure and simple refrain strongly suggest a long tradition of popular poetry which may, if we accept the evidence of Hattian
texts which seem to show some sort of stanza-division, go back to the pre-
Hittite period. None of it, however, with the exception of this fragment,
has been preserved. But when we remember that a song sung by Julius
Caesar's soldiers is practically the only evidence preserved in 'literary'
Latin for a vast undercurrent of Roman popular song whose characteristic features did not come fully to the surface until the medieval period, it is
easy to believe that a similarly large body of material existed in second-
millennium Anatolia. But since it was of little interest to the staff of the
temples and chancellery it was not normally recorded in writing and has
now been irretrievably lost.

With literature we conclude our survey of the Anatolian Late Bronze
Age. If the account has been dominated by the Hittites this reflects not
only the comparative lack of material from other areas, but also the
dominant position which they held at the time. Their rediscovery has
revealed to us a people who, if they did not possess the genius and
originality to change the course of world history, at least showed a
talent for political and military organization, and a capacity to utilize
their resources, which enabled them to gain, and retain for several
hundred years, a leading position in the Middle Eastern world. Equally
important, it has enabled us to see them not merely as remote people in a
remote world but as real human beings with a personality and an
individuality which we can still recognize after more than three thousand
years.

Notes

For abbreviations see Bibliography, p. 153.

1 The type-site is Arpachiyah, near Mosul. See M. E. L. Mallowan and J. Cruikshank Rose, *Prehistoric Assyria, The Excavations at Tell Arpachiyah* (1935). For a comparison with Anatolia cf. J. Mellaart, *CAH* I, 1, 281.

2 See for instance the development at Eridu. S. Lloyd and F. Safar, *Sumer* IV (1948) 115 sqq.; S. Lloyd, *ILN*, May 31, 1947, 581 sqq.; *ILN* Sept. 11, 1948, 303 ff.

3 H. Frankfort, *The Art and Architecture of the Ancient Orient* (1970), 211 ff.

4 C. L. Woolley, *Ur Excavations*, Vol. II, *The Royal Cemetery* (1934). See also the same author's *Ur of the Chaldees* (1929), *Excavations at Ur* (1954) and other publications.

5 M. E. L. Mallowan, Excavations at Brak and Chagar Bazar; *Iraq* 9 (1947), 1 ff.

6 L. R. Palmer, *Mycenaeans and Minoans* (1965), 246 ff.

7 M. J. Mellink in R. W. Ehrich, *Chronologies in Old World Archaeology* (1965), 115 ff.

8 C. J. Gadd in *CAH* I, 2, 426 ff.

9 J. Mellaart, *AJA* 62 (1958), 14.

10 The arrival of this pottery in central Anatolia has also been equated with that of Hittite-speakers. Cf. J. Mellaart, *CAH* I, 2, 694; R. A. Crossland, *ibid.* 845.

11 W. F. Albright and T. O. Lambdin, *CAH* I, 1, 142.

12 J. Mellaart, *AJA* 62 (1958) 20–21.

13 R. J. Howell in R. A. Crossland and A. Birchell (eds) *Bronze Age Migrations in the Aegean* (1973), 73 ff.

14 D. H. French, *AnSt* XVII (1967), 62–3.

15 J. B. Haley and C. W. Blegen, The Coming of the Greeks; *AJA* XXXII (1928), 141 ff.

16 Cf. M. B. Rowton, *CAH* I, 1, 212 ff. The literature on the subject is extensive.

17 J. Mellaart, Anatolian Trade with Europe and Anatolian Geography and Culture Provinces in the Late Bronze Age. *AnSt* XVIII (1968), 187 ff.

18 Contact is shown by the presence of 'ingot-torcs', riveted daggers and other features in both regions. See S. Piggott, *Ancient Europe* (1965), 102 and Fig. 56.

19 J. Garstang and O. R. Gurney, *The Geography of the Hittite Empire* (1959), 73. For alternative locations see K. Bittel, *Hattusha* (1970), 21; E. Laroche, *AJA* 78 (1974), 111.

20 For recent accounts of the battle see Y. Yadin, *The Art of Warfare in Biblical Lands* (1963), 103 ff.; C. W. Ceram, *Narrow Pass, Black Mountain* (1956), 160 ff.

21 For recent treatments of the subject of the Sea Peoples see V. Hankey, *Asian Affairs* NS V (1974), 51 ff.; J. Mellaart, Western Anatolia, Beycesultan and the Hittites, *Mansel'e Armağan (Melanges Mansel)*, (1974), 493 ff.

22 The idea of a Hittite monopoly of iron comes from an unwarranted interpretation of a Hittite document (*KBo* I, 14) which

mentions a request for iron made by a foreign monarch. For details of the text see A. Goetze, *Kizzuwatna and the Problem of Hittite Geography* (1940), 27–33.

23 R. S. Young, *AJA* LXII (1958), 139 ff.

24 (a) H. Goldman, *AJA* XLI (1937), 284.
(b) H. Goldman, *Excavations at Gözlü Kule, Tarsus*, II, (1956), 29.

25 C. W. Blegen, *Troy and the Trojans* (1963), 154.

26 K. Bittel, *Hattusha* (1970), 85.

27 F. Fischer, *Die hethitische Keramik von Bogazköy* (1963), 32.

28 C. A. Burney and D. M. Lang, *The Peoples of the Hills* (1971), 47, 86.

29 J. Mellaart, *AnSt* V (1955), 53. The suggestion is made for south-western pottery, but is equally apt for north-western vessels.

30 H. G. Güterbock, *JNES* XX (1961), 93.

31 Location on Halys: J. Garstang and O. R. Gurney, *The Geography of the Hittite Empire* (1959), 36; on Euphrates: S. Alp, Die Lage von Šamuḫa, *Anatolia* I (1956), 77 ff.

32 Y. Yadin, *The Art of Warfare in Biblical Lands* (1963), 3.

33 C. W. Blegen, *Troy* III, i (1953), 96.

34 P. Stirling, *Turkish Village* (1965); J. E. Pierce, *Life in a Turkish Village* (1964).

35 L. R. Palmer, *Achaeans and Indo-Europeans* (1955), 14; O. R. Gurney, *CAH* II, 1, 253 ff. For another view see S. Piggott, *Ancient Europe* (1965), 81.

36 J. G. Macqueen, *AnSt* IX (1959), 181; O. R. Gurney, *CAH* II, 1, 667 ff.

37 J. G. Macqueen, *op. cit.* 179.

38 K. Bittel, *Hattusha* (1970), 107–8.

39 K. Bittel, *op. cit.* 110.

40 O. R. Gurney, *The Hittites* (1952) 164 ff.

41 G. Daux, *Bulletin de Correspondence Hellénique* XCII (1968), 1038 f. (Argos). Cremation-burial is also attested in the Middle Bronze Age Age in Epirus (N. G. L. Hammond, *Epirus* (1967), 229), and in the Early Bronze Age on Leukas (W. Dörpfeld, *Alt-Ithaka* (1927); J. L. Caskey, *CAH* I, 2, 792–3).

42 Traces of wall-painting are now reported from Maşat Hüyük near Zile (*AJA* 78 (1974), 110.

43 S. Lloyd, *Early Highland Peoples of Anatolia* (1967), 64–5.

44 K. Bittel, *Hattusha* (1970), 98.

Select Bibliography

This list is not intended to be an exhaustive bibliography of Hittite studies, but rather an introductory selection of books and articles dealing with subjects and problems mentioned in the text. Many of the works mentioned contain further bibliographies which should be consulted by anyone who wishes to go into greater detail or make up his own mind on controversial points.

ABBREVIATIONS

AfO	*Archiv für Orientforschung*
AJA	*American Journal of Archaeology*
AnSt	*Anatolian Studies*
Bell	Türk Tarih Kurumu: *Belleten*
BMQ	*British Museum Quarterly*
CAH	*Cambridge Ancient History*
ILN	*Illustrated London News*
JAOS	*Journal of the American Oriental Society*
JCS	*Journal of Cuneiform Studies*
JNES	*Journal of Near Eastern Studies*
KBo	*Keilschrifttexte aus Boghazköi*
KUB	*Keilschrifturkunden aus Boghazköi*
MDOG	*Mitteilungen der deutschen Orientgesellschaft*
OLZ	*Orientalistische Literaturzeitung*
RHA	*Revue Hittite et Asianique*
ScAm	*Scientific American*
TAD	*Türk Arkeoloji Dergisi*
TTKR	*Türk Tarih Kurumu Raporlari*
ZA	*Zeitschrift für Assyriologie*

GENERAL

ALKIM, U. B. *Anatolia* I. London, 1969.

BITTEL, K. *Hattusha, Capital of the Hittites.* New York, 1970.

Cambridge Ancient History, 3rd edn, Cambridge, Vol. I, 1 1970; Vol. I, 2 1971; Vol. II, 1 1973; Vol. II, 2 forthcoming.

GOETZE, A. *Kleinasien.* 2nd edn, Munich, 1957.

GURNEY, O. R. *The Hittites.* Harmondsworth and San Francisco 1952 and subsequent editions.

LLOYD, S. *Early Anatolia.* Harmondsworth, 1956.

— *Early Highland Peoples of Anatolia.* London and New York, 1967.

OTTEN, H. Das Hethiterreich, in Schmökel, H. *Kulturgeschichte des alten Orient.* Stuttgart, 1961.

PRITCHARD, J. B. (ed.) *Ancient Near Eastern Texts Relating to the Old Testament.* Princeton, 1950, 1955, 1969.

SCHMÖKEL, H. *Geschichte des alten Vorderasien,* pp. 119–70. Leiden, 1957.

WALSER G. (ed.) *Neuere Hethiterforschung* (*Historia*: Einzelschriften 7). Wiesbaden, 1964.

Summaries of archaeological work and preliminary reports of excavations appear in *AJA, AnSt, TAD, TTKR, Bell, MDOG, Orientalia, Anatolica, Anadolu (Anatolia), Jahrbericht Ex Oriente Lux.* Many other periodicals (e.g. *RHA, JAOS, JCS, JNES, ZA*) contain articles dealing with Anatolian topics.

CHAPTER I

ARIK, R. O. *Les Fouilles d' Alaca Höyük, 1935.* Ankara, 1936.

BRICE, W. C. *South-West Asia.* London, 1966. Vol. 8 in Systematic Regional Geography Series, ed. J. F. Unstead. (Excellent on geography of Turkey.)

BURNEY, C. A. and LANG, D. M. *The Peoples of the Hills; Ancient Ararat and Caucasus.* London and New York, 1971.

ÇAMBEL, H. and BRAIDWOOD, R. J. *An Early Farming Village in Turkey. ScAm* March 1970, 50–6.

COHEN, H. The Palaeoecology of South Central Anatolia at the End of the Pleistocene and the Beginning of the Holocene. *AnSt* XX (1970), 119–37.

FORBES, R. J. *Studies in Ancient Technology,* VIII–IX. *(Metallurgy in Antiquity).* Leiden, 1964.

GARELLI, P. *Les Assyriens en Cappadoce.* Paris, 1963.

GARSTANG, J. *Prehistoric Mersin.* Oxford and New York, 1953.

GÜTERBOCK, H. G. Die historische Tradi-tion und ihre literarische Gestaltung bei Babyloniern und Hethitern bis 1200. *ZA* 42 (1934), 1 ff., and 44 (1938), 45 ff.

— Kaneš and Neša, Two Forms of One Anatolian Name. *Eretz-Israel* V, (1958), 46–50.

KOŞAY, H. Z. *Ausgrabungen von Alaca Höyük.* Ankara, 1944.

— *Les Fouilles d'Alaca Höyük, 1937–39.* Ankara, 1951.

LLOYD, S. and MELLAART, J. *Beycesultan.* London, Vol. I, 1962; Vol. II, 1965.

MELLAART, J. *Çatal Hüyük. A Neolithic Town in Anatolia.* London and New York, 1967.

— *The Chalcolithic and Early Bronze Ages in the Near East and Anatolia.* Beirut, 1966.

— *Earliest Civilizations of the Near East.* London and New York, 1965.

— Excavations at Çatal Hüyük. *AnSt* XII (1962), 41–65; XIII (1963), 43–103; XIV (1964), 39–119; XVI (1966), 165–91.

— *Hacilar.* Edinburgh, 1970.

— The Royal Treasure of Dorak. *ILN* 28 Nov. 1959.

ORLIN, L. L. *Assyrian Colonies in Cappodocia.* The Hague, 1970.

OTTEN, H. Zu den Anfangen der Hethiti-schen Geschichte. *MDOG* 83 (1951), 33–45.

ÖZGÜÇ, N. *The Anatolian Group of Cylinder Impressions from Kültepe.* Ankara, 1965.

— Marble Idols and Statuettes from the Excavations at Kültepe. *Bell* XXI (1957), 71–80.

ÖZGÜÇ, T. The Art and Architecture of Ancient Kanesh. *Anatolia* VIII (1964), 27–48.

— An Assyrian Trading Outpost. *ScAm*

Feb. 1963, 97–106.
— *Ausgrabungen in Kültepe, 1948.* Ankara, 1950.
— The Dagger of Anitta. *Bell* XX (1956), 33–36.
— *Kültepe-Kaniş; New Researches at the Center of the Assyrian Trade Colonies.* Ankara, 1959.
ÖZGÜÇ, T. and N. *Ausgrabungen in Kültepe, 1949.* Ankara, 1953.
RYAN, C. W. *A Guide to the Known Minerals of Turkey.* Ankara, 1960.
SCHLIEMANN, H. *Troy and its Remains.* London, 1875.
— *Ilios the City of the Trojans.* London and New York, 1880.
— *Troja: Results of the Latest Researches and Discoveries on the Site of Homer's Troy.* London and New York, 1884.
TODD, I. A. Aşikli Hüyük. *AnSt* XVI (1966), 139–63.
TODD, I. A. and PASQUARE, G. The Chipped Stone Industry of Avla Dağ. *AnSt* XV (1965), 95–112.
UCKO, P. J. and DIMBLEBY, G. W. (eds). *The Domestication and Exploitation of Plants and Animals.* London and Chicago, 1969.

CHAPTER II
CROSSLAND, R. A. Immigrants from the North. *CAH* I, 2, 824 ff.
CROSSLAND, R. A. and BIRCHALL, A. *Bronze Age Migrations in the Aegean.* London and Park Ridge, 1973 and 1974.
FRENCH, D. H. Prehistoric Sites in N-W Anatolia. *AnSt* XVII (1967), esp. 61–4.
FRIEDRICH, J. *Hethitisches Elementarbuch* I–II. Heidelberg, 1946–60.
— *Hethitisches Keilschriftlesebuch.* Heidel-
berg, 1960.
— *Hethitisches Wörterbuch.* Heidelberg, 1952 and supplements.
GIMBUTAS, M. The Indo-Europeans: Archaeological Problems. *American Anthropologist* 65 (1963), 815 ff.
— Proto-Indo-European Culture, in *Indo-European and Indo-Europeans.* Philadelphia, 1970.
HROZNÝ, B. *Die Lösung des Hethitischen Problems.* Leipzig, 1915.
— *Die Sprache der Hethiter.* Leipzig. 1917.
KNUDTZON J. A. *Die zwei Arzawa-Briefe: die ältesten Urkunden in indo-germanischer Sprache.* Leipzig, 1902.
LAROCHE, E. *Dictionnaire de la Langue Louvite.* Paris, 1959.
— *Les Hiéroglyphes Hittites,* Vol. I. Paris, 1960.
MACQUEEN, J. G. The First Arrival of Indo-European Elements in Greece. Some Obserservations from Anatolia, in *Acta of the 2nd International Colloquium on Aegean Prehistory.* Athens, 1972.
MELLAART, J. The End of the Early Bronze Age in Anatolia and the Aegean. *AJA* 62 (1958), 9–33.
MELLINK, M. J. Anatolian Chronology, in Ehrich, R. W. (ed.) *Chronologies in Old World Archaeology.* Chicago, 1965.
PALMER, L. R. *Mycenaeans and Minoans.* London and New York, 1965.
SAYCE, A. H. On the Hamathite Inscriptions. *Transactions of the Society for Biblical Archaeology,* V. 1877.
— The Hittites in Asia Minor. *Academy,* Aug. 16, 1879.
— The Monuments of the Hittites. *Transactions of the Society for Biblical Archaeology,* VII. 1882.

STURTEVANT, E. H. *A Comparative Grammar of the Hittite Language.* 2nd edn Philadelphia, 1951.
— *A Hittite Chrestomathy.* Philadelphia, 1935.

CHAPTER III

AKURGAL, E. *Phrygische Kunst.* Ankara, 1955.

ASTOUR, M. C. *Hellenosemitica.* Leiden, 1965.

FORRER, E. O. Die Griechen in den Boghazköi-Texten. *OLZ* 1924, 113–18.
— Vorhomerische Griechen in den Keilschrifttexten von Boghazköi. *MDOG* 63 (1924), 1–22.

GARSTANG, J. and GURNEY, O. R. *The Geography of the Hittite Empire.* London, 1959.

GOETZE, A. *Die Annalen des Mursilis.* Leipzig, 1933.
— *Hattusilis.* Leipzig, 1925.
— *Hattusilis. Neue Bruchstücke.* Leipzig, 1930.
— *Madduwattaš.* Leipzig, 1928.
— The Predecessors of Šuppiluliumaš of Hatti. *JOAS* 72 (1952), 67 ff.
— The Roads of Northern Cappodocia in Hittite Times. *RHA* 61 (1957), 91 ff.

GÜTERBOCK, H. G. The Deeds of Suppiluliuma, as Told by his Son Mursili II. *JCS* 10 (1956), 41 ff.
— Hattušili II Once More. *JCS* 25 (1973), 100–4.
— The Hittite Conquest of Cyprus Reconsidered. *JNES* 26 (1967), 73–81.
— The North-Central Area of Hittite Anatolia. *JNES* 20 (1961), 88 ff.
— The Predecessors of Suppiluliuma Again. *JNES* 29 (1970), 73–7.

HAUSCHILD, R. *Die indogermanischer Völker und Sprachen Kleinasiens.* Berlin, 1964.

HOUWINK TEN CATE P. H. J. *Kleinasien zwischen Hethitern und Persern.* Frankfurt, 1967.
— *The Luwian Population Groups of Lycia and Cilicia Aspera during the Hellenistic Period.* Leiden, 1961.
— *The Records of the Early Hittite Empire.* Leiden, 1970.

HUXLEY, G. L. *Achaeans and Hittites.* Oxford, 1960.

LAROCHE, E. *Catalogue des Textes Hittites.* Paris, 1971.

LUCKENBILL, D. D. *Ancient Records of Assyria and Babylonia* II. Chicago 1927.

MACQUEEN, J. G. Geography and History in Western Asia Minor in the Second Millenium B.C. *AnSt* XVIII (1968), 169 ff.

MELLAART, J. Anatolian Trade with Europe and Anatolian Geography and Culture Provinces in the Late Bronze Age. *AnSt* XVIII (1968), 187 ff.

NEUMANN, G. *Untersuchungen zum Weiterleben hethitischen u. luwischen Sprachgutes in hellenistischer u. römischer Zeit.* Weisbaden, 1961.

OTTEN, H. *Die hethitischen historischen Quellen u. die altorientalisçhe Chronologie.* Wiesbaden, 1968.
— Neue Quellen zum Ausklang der Hethitischen Geschichte. *MDOG* 94 (1963), 1–23.
— *MDOG* 91 (1958), 75–84. (Historical text of Hattusilis I.)

PAGE, D. L. *History and the Homeric Iliad.* Berkeley, 1959.

SOMMER, F. *Die Ahhijavá-Urkunden.* Munich, 1932.

SCHULER, E. VON. *Die Kaškäer: Ein Beitrag zur Ethnographie des alten Kleinasien.* Berlin, 1965.

STEINER, G. Die Ahhijawa-Frage heute. *Saeculum* 15 (1964), 365–92.

YOUNG, R. S. Reports on Gordion excavations in *AJA* 59 (1955) and subsequent volumes.

CHAPTER IV

BARNETT, R. D. Ancient Oriental Gold-work. *BMQ* XXII, 1, 2 (1960), 29 ff.

BASS, G. *Cape Gelidonya: a Bronze Age Shipwreck.* Philadelphia, 1967.

BERAN, T. *Die hethitische Glyptik von Boğaz-köy.* Berlin, 1967.

BITTEL, K. and GÜTERBOCK, H. G. *Boğaz-köy. Neue Untersuchungen in der Hethitischen Hauptstadt.* Berlin, 1935.

BITTEL, K. and NAUMANN, R. *Boğazköy II. Neue Untersuchungen hethitischer Architektur.* Berlin, 1938.

— *Boğazköy-Hattuša I. Architektur, Topographie, Landeskunde u. Siedlungsgeschichte.* Stuttgart, 1952.

BITTEL, K., NAUMANN, R. *et al. Boğazköy III. Funde aus den Grabungen 1952–55.* Berlin, 1957.

BLEGEN, C. W. *et al. Troy.* Princeton, Vol. III, 1953; Vol. IV, 1958.

BOEHMER, R. M. *Die Kleinfunde von Boğazköy.* Berlin, 1972.

BURNEY, C. A. Northern Anatolia before Classical Times. *AnSt* VI (1956), 179 ff.

FISCHER, F. *Die hethitische Keramik von Boğazköy.* Berlin, 1963.

FRENCH, D. H. Prehistoric Sites in N-W Anatolia. I *AnSt* XVII (1967), 49–100; II *AnSt* XIX (1969), 41–98.

GOETZE, A. Hittite Dress. *Corolla Linguistica.* Wiesbaden, 1955.

GOLDMAN, H. *Excavations at Gözlü Kule, Tarsus,* II. Princeton, 1956.

GÜTERBOCK, H. G. *Siegel aus Boğazköy.* Berlin. Vol. I 1940; Vol. II 1942.

KADISH, B. Prehistoric Aphrodisias. *AJA* 75 (1971), 121–40.

KOŞAY, H. Z. and AKOK, M. *Ausgrabungen von Alaca Höyük 1940–1948.* Ankara, 1966.

LAMB, W. Excavations at Kusura near Afyon Karahisar. *Archaeologia* 86 (1936) 1–64; 87 (1937), 217–74.

— *Excavations at Thermi in Lesbos.* Cambridge and New York, 1936.

LLOYD, S. *Beycesultan* III, i. London, 1972.

LLOYD, S. and MELLAART, J. Beycesultan Excavations; First Preliminary Report. *AnSt* V (1955), 39–93. Second Preliminary Report. *AnSt* VI (1956), 101–35.

MAXWELL-HYSLOP, R. *Western Asiatic Jewellery c. 3000–612 B.C.* London and New York, 1971.

MELLAART, J. The Second Millennium Chronology of Beycesultan. *AnSt* XX (1970), 55–67.

Middle East Technical University. Keban Project Reports. I–. 1968–.

NAUMANN, R. *Architektur Kleinasiens.* 2nd edn. Tübingen, 1971.

ORTHMANN, W. *Frühe Keramik von Boğazköy.* Berlin, 1963.

ÖZGÜÇ, T. The Bitik Vase. *Anatolia* II (1957), 57–78.

— New Finds from Horoztepe. *Anatolia* VIII (1964), 1 ff.

ÖZGÜÇ, T. and N. *Ausgrabungen in Karahüyük 1947.* Ankara, 1949.

SCHAEFFER, C. F. A. *et al. Ugaritica* III.

Paris, 1956.

SCHIRMER, W. *Die Bebauung am unteren Büyükkale-Nordwesthang in Boğazköy.* Berlin, 1969.

SEIDL, U. *Gefässmarken von Boğazköy.* Berlin, 1972.

CHAPTER V

GOETZE, A. Warfare in Asia Minor. *Iraq* 25 (1963), 124 ff.

MAXWELL-HYSLOP, R. Daggers and Swords in Western Asia. *Iraq* VIII (1946), 1–65.

— Western Asiatic Shaft-Hole Axes. *Iraq* XI (1949), 90–129.

OSTEN, H. H. VON DER. *The Alishar Huyuk. Seasons of 1930–32,* Part II. Chicago, 1937.

PUCHSTEIN, O. *Boghasköi, Die Bauwerke.* Leipzig, 1912.

STRONACH, D. The Development and Diffusion of Metal Types in Early Bronze Age Anatolia. *AnSt* VII (1957), 89–125.

YADIN, Y. *The Art of Warfare in Biblical Lands.* London, 1963.

CHAPTER VI

FRIEDRICH, J. *Die hethitischen Gesetze.* Leiden, 1959.

— *Staatsverträge des Hatti-Reiches in Hethitischer Sprache.* Leipzig, 1926–30.

GURNEY, O. R. Hittite Kingship, in Hooke, S. H. (ed.), *Myth, Ritual and Kingship.* Oxford and New York, 1958.

GÜTERBOCK, H. G. Authority and Law in the Hittite Kingdom. *JAOS* Suppl. 17 (1954), 16–24.

SCHULER, E. VON. Hethitische Dienstanweisungen für Höhere Hof- und Staats-

beamte. *AfO,* Beiheft 10, 1957.

WEIDNER, E. F. *Politische Dokumente aus Kleinasien.* Leipzig, 1923.

CHAPTER VII

BITTEL, K. *et al. Die hethitischen Grabfunde von Osmankayasi.* Berlin, 1958.

— *Yazilikaya, Architektur, Felsbilder, Inschriften und Kleinfunde.* Leipzig, 1941.

GURNEY, O. R. Hittite Prayers of Mursili II. *Annals of Archaeology and Anthropology* 27. Liverpool, 1940.

GÜTERBOCK, H. G. Hittite Religion, in Ferm, V., *Forgotten Religions.* New York, 1949.

—— An Outline of the Hittite AN.TAH.ŠUM Festival. *JNES* XIX (1960), 80 ff.

LAROCHE, E. Le Panthéon de Yazilikaya. *JCS* VI (1952), 114–23.

MACQUEEN, J. G. Hattian Mythology and Hittite Monarchy. *AnSt* IX (1959), 171–88.

MELLINK, M. J. *A Hittite Cemetery at Gordion.* Philadelphia, 1956.

ORTHMANN, W. *Das Gräberfeld bei Ilica.* Wiesbaden, 1967.

OTTEN, H. *Hethitische Totenrituale.* Berlin, 1958.

CHAPTER VIII

AKURGAL, E. *The Art of the Hittites.* London and New York, 1962.

BOSSERT, H. T. *Altanatolien.* Berlin, 1942.

FRANKFORT, H. A. *The Art and Architecture of the Ancient Orient.* 4th edn. Harmondsworth, 1970.

GÜTERBOCK, H. G. The Composition of

Hittite Prayers to the Sun. *JAOS* 78 (1958), 237 ff.

— Hittite Mythology, in Kramer, S. N. (ed.), *Mythologies of the Ancient World.* New York, 1961.

— The Hittite Version of the Hurrian Kumarbi Myths; Oriental Forerunners of Hesoid. *AJA* 52 (1948), 123 ff.

— Notes on some Hittite Monuments. *AnSt*

VI (1956), 53 ff.

— *The Song of Ullikummi.* New Haven, 1952.

MCNEILL, I. The Metre of the Hittite Epic. *AnSt* XIII (1963), 237 ff.

RIEMSCHNEIDER, M. *Die Welt der Hethiter.* 5th edn. Stuttgart, 1965.

VIEYRA, M. *Hittite Art, 2300–750 B.C.* London and Hollywood-by-the-sea, 1955.

1

2

3

4

5

6

9

10

11

12

MANGER ROOM   STREET   COURT

NORTH ROOM

RAMP

13

14

15

17

a

b

18

c

d

e

19

21

22

23

24

25

26

27

28

29

31

30

32

33

34

35

36

37

38

39

40

41

42

43

44

45

46

47

48

49

50

51

52

53

54

55

56

57

58

59

60

61

62

63

64

65

67

66

68

Notes on the Plates

1 View from the Lion Gate, Boğazköy. The photograph shows the typically bare central Anatolian hill-country which lies south of the capital. In Hittite times much of it must have been thickly wooded.

2 Spear-head found at Kültepe, with inscription reading 'Palace of Anita, the king'. The bent tang has been broken, and the two holes through which the head was bound to the shaft have apparently been wrongly placed, filled in, and remade further down. Length 9 in. Archaeological Museum, Ankara.

3 Rock relief at Gavurkalesi near Ankara. Two gods face a seated goddess. Behind the relief lies a tomb-chamber which may once have contained the remains of a local monarch.

4 Rock relief at Karabel, east of Izmir. This relief has been taken to be a monument of Hittite conquest in the west, but is more probably the work of a local king.

5 This copy of a detail from an Egyptian relief shows Rameses II exhibiting his skill during the Battle of Qadesh. Mail-clad Hittites fall before his skilful archery. Reliefs such as this one give a great deal of information on weapons and chariots.

6 Many details of the weapons and equipment of the 'Sea Peoples' can be seen in this reconstruction of an Egyptian relief. Their ships have battering rams shaped like ducks' bills and, unlike the Egyptian vessels, do not have oars. Three ships carry Philistines, recognizable by their feather-topped helmets, while the other two are manned by another people, distinguished by their helmets with horns. All carry round shields and long straight swords. Some at least of the Sea Peoples may have come from Anatolia.

7 The 'North Street' area of Beycesultan II, facing east. The surface of the street can be clearly seen. On the left is a building of megaron type with circular hearth, approached through a room in which a paved area may have been used for ablutions. Beyond the east end of the megaron lie the grain-shop and tavern. To the right of the street lie the stables.

8 Drainage-channel running along the front of Temple I, Boğazköy.

9 The stone sink in the 'snack bar' of Troy VIIa. The bottom is formed of thin stone slabs and the sides of similar stone slabs standing on edge and rising about six inches above the level of the bottom. A rectangular hole in the wall of the building, seen at the bottom left-hand corner of the sink, allows water to drain into the street outside. Since the joints of the slabs are not waterproofed it is possible that jars of water were stood on the paving and that the drain was provided to cope only with leakages or spilt liquid.

10 A view of the 'snack bar' of Troy VIIa, with the stone sink in the foreground and an oven, hearth and large saddle-quern in the background. The walls at the rear are of Roman date.

11 Bath-tub from Alaca. H. 30 in. L. 29 in.

12 Street in Tarsus LB II, looking south, with the 'Governor's Residence' on the left.

13 A view from the east over the stables at Beycesultan II, with 'North Street' on the right. Against the wall in front of the standing figure on the right of the photograph was a large

manger, and the floor around it was covered with straw in which the footprints of horses could still be seen. The rectangular area in the centre (behind the head of the sitting figure) was a pit for the disposal of manure, while further back can be seen three small semicircular areas of destruction-deposit left in position to preserve the impressions of three tethering-posts.

14 The grain-shop at Beycesultan II, and the tavern behind. The storage jars built into the bar of the latter can be clearly seen.

15 View to the north-west from the citadel of Boğazköy. The deep gorge which protects the citadel can be seen in the centre of the picture, with the dragon's-head rock known as Büyük-kaya, which just before the final fall of Hattusas was enclosed by an extension of the city walls, across the gorge on the right. Beyond the city to the north is the fertile agricultural country which must have provided much of the capital's food.

16 Tools and agricultural implements. *a*, Sickle from Tarsus: L. 10½ in. *b*, Bronze hammer from Alaca: L. 5 in. *c*, Chisel from Mersin. *d*, Chisel from Tarsus: L. 9 in. *e*, Chisel from Alaca: L. 8 in. *f*, Builder's trowel (?)

from Alaca: L. 3¾ in. *g*, Hoe from Mersin.

17 Steatite mould from Troy VIIa, broken at one end. On one side are the matrices for two ring-shaped pendants and three small spherical beads. On the other the matrices are for four ring-pendants and three slender segmented beads. L. 3¼ in.

18 Amulets and figurines. *a*, from Boğaz-köy; *b*, from Ugarit; *c*, from Troy; *d*, in the British Museum; *e*, from Boğazköy. Not to scale.

19 *a*, Impression of a gold signet-ring, now in the Ashmolean Museum, Oxford. *b*, impression of a cylinder-seal from Kültepe, showing the god Pirwa standing on a four-wheeled chariot drawn by four horses. Facing him is the god Adad standing on a lion-dragon and holding a spear and a thunderbolt. A human figure lies prostrate under the chariot.

20 Seals. Top row, from Boğazköy. Centre row, *(l. to r.)* seal of Isputahsu, from Tarsus; from Boğazköy; seal of Mursilis III (Urhi-Teshub), from Boğazköy. Bottom row, *(l. to r.)* seals of Suppiluliumas and Queen Tawanannas, of Tudhaliyas IV, and of Ini-Teshub, king of Carchemish, from Ugarit. Not to scale.

21 Fragment of a vessel with decoration in relief, from Bitik near Ankara. The top scene, where a man lifts a woman's veil and offers her a bowl, probably has a religious significance (a sacred marriage?). The central register shows a procession of worshippers, while below it the remains of two figures can be seen, perhaps performing a religi-ous dance with daggers. Height of fragment 15 in. Archaeological Mu-seum, Ankara.

22 Pair of ritual bull-vases from Boğaz-köy. H. 36 in. Archaeological Mu-seum, Ankara.

23 Pottery from Beycesultan Level II, showing the characteristic 'chalices' and 'fruit-stands'.

24 Weapons. *(l. to r.)* sword from Thermi, L. 14 in.; knife from Alaca, L. 10 in.; arrowhead from Thermi, L. 2¼ in.; flat axe from Alaca, L. 11 in.; arrowhead from Mersin; socketed spearhead from Tarsus, L. 12 in.; dagger from Tarsus, L. 7½ in.

25 Part of the Late Bronze Age wall of Tarsus, showing the large stones typical of Hittite masonry.

26 This fragment of the rim of a Hittite vessel is our best evidence for the towers and battlements of Hittite fortifications. Note the imitation

wooden beams protruding from the tower. H. 4¼ in. Archaeological Museum, Ankara.

27 The Lion Gate, Boğazköy.

28 A section of the city wall of Troy VI, showing the characteristic vertical 'offsets', about thirty feet apart, each marking a slight change in the direction of the wall.

29 The East Gate, Troy VI, showing the narrow passage formed by two overlapping sections of the wall.

30 House in Troy VIIa, with storage vessels sunk into the floor. It is often held that the number of such vessels in the houses of Troy VIIa shows that the settlement was in a state of siege, and that the attackers were the Greeks of the Homeric poems.

31 The pillars set up outside the South Gate, Troy VI. Probably originally six in number, they may well have had some sort of protective function.

32 The spring sanctuary at Eflatun Pinar, near Beyşehir. The platform originally had two large figures on it, either incorporating the Fassilar statue (as shown in Fig. 36), or with two seated figures which were larger versions of those in relief on the lower

face of the platform. The natural pool in front of the platform was enlarged in the Hittite period by a dam with a sluice.

33 Rock relief at Sirkeli near Adana, with figure of Muwatallis.

34 Ritual structure, with hearth and 'horns', in the Level III shrine at Beycesultan.

35 Ritual structure, with hearth and 'horns', in the Level II shrine at Beycesultan.

36 Remains of structure in an apparently domestic context (Level II) at Beycesultan. The rectangular pillar originally supported a cooking pot, and 'horns' similar to those seen in Plate 34 can perhaps be restored to the left of it.

37 View from the citadel at Boğazköy, looking north-west over Temple I. The main temple-building with its surrounding store-rooms can be clearly seen.

38 The entrance to the main building of Temple I. Note the low sills of the large windows on either side of the doorway.

39 A stone pedestal with a scene on the

side showing a worshipper before a similar base topped by an upright stele. This is probably the cult-object referred to in the texts as a *huwasi*-stone, and a similar object may well have stood on the pedestal itself. H. $36\frac{1}{2}$ in. Archaeological Museum of Istanbul.

40 The entrance to the underground pool in the main temple-complex at Boğaz-köy. The right-hand part of the broken lintel, seen restored to its original position, has the figure of a worshipper incised on it.

41 The inner part of the underground pool, showing the corbel-vaulting and the rear wall. Water entered the pool through the space beneath the smaller stone in the third row from the bottom.

42 The 'crematory' at Troy VI. The spaces between the three brick piers may have been stoke-holes or air-vents for a furnace in which bodies were burned.

43 An intra-mural burial at Boğazköy. A large pottery vessel has been cut in two vertically to provide a cover for the body.

44 A view of Yazilikaya from the south-east, showing the remains of the temple buildings and the outer part of Chamber A.

45 Chamber A at Yazilikaya, showing the rear part of the procession of male deities.

46 The central group of figures in Chamber A at Yazilikaya.

47 The figure of King Tudhaliyas, which stands at the rear of the female procession in Chamber A at Yazili-kaya.

48 A view of Chamber B at Yazilikaya, showing the narrowness of the cham-ber and the great size of the sculptures in it.

49 The 'sword god' in Chamber B at Yazilikaya.

50 Tudhaliyas in the embrace of his protective deity. Chamber B at Yazi-likaya.

51 The 'soldier-gods' in Chamber B at Yazilikaya.

52 A lion holding a calf, from Alaca. This was probably a portal-figure, but its original position is uncertain. H. 3 ft 3 in. Archaeological Museum, Ankara.

53 A front view of the group shown in Plate 52. Note the formalized decora-tion on the calf.

The Hittites

54 A king and queen worshipping a deity in the form of a bull, from Alaca. H. 4 ft 2 in. Archaeological Museum, Ankara.

55 A group of acrobats, from Alaca. The figure on the right is climbing an unsupported ladder, while the one on the left is a sword-swallower. H. 3 ft 10 in. Archaeological Museum, Ankara.

56 A musician, and a man carrying an animal (a dog or monkey?), from Alaca. H. 3 ft 10 in. Archaeological Museum, Ankara.

57 A hunting scene from Alaca. The blocks bearing hunting scenes probably formed a row immediately above the procession of worshippers, acrobats and musicians. H. 4 ft 4 in. Archaeological Museum, Ankara.

58 Lion-hunting with dogs, from Alaca. H. 4 ft 3 in. Archaeological Museum, Ankara.

59 Stag-hunt from Alaca. H. 2 ft 8 in. Archaeological Museum, Ankara.

60 Left-hand end of rock relief at Fraktin, showing Hattusilis III offering a libation to the storm-god. Height of figures 4 ft 4 in.

61 Right-hand end of rock-relief at Fraktin, showing Queen Puduhepa offering a libation to the goddess Hepat. Height of figures 4 ft 4 in.

62 The figure from the left-hand inner side of the King's Gate, Boğazköy. Height of figure 6 ft 6 in. Archaeological Museum, Ankara.

63 One of the figures from the Sphinx Gate, Boğazköy.

64 The right-hand figure of the Lion Gate, Boğazköy.

65 The Sphinx Gate, Alaca. A double-headed eagle, on which a long-robed human figure is standing, can be seen on the inner side of the right-hand figure.

66 Bronze statuette of a god, from Tokat. The horns attached to the head rather than to the hat, and the position of the right arm, show that this figure does not conform completely to the Hittite tradition. H. $4\frac{1}{2}$ in. Archaeological Museum, Ankara.

67 Bronze statuette, from Boğazköy. This figure conforms more than that in Plate 66 to the canons of Hittite art. H. 5 in.

68 A bronze rein-ring surmounted by a man and rearing horse. From Yozgat, now in the Louvre.

Photographic Acknowledgments

Index

9/02
3 clics
lost 1 mt
3/02

KEY

- ancient site
- ○ modern town
- ◉ ancient site/modern town
- (Kanesh) Hittite name for site

Black Sea

İstanbul

S. of Marmara

L. Apolyont

İnand

Troy

Sakarya

Ankara

Porsuk Çay

Gordion

İlıca

Polatlı

Gâvurkal

Lesbos

Salt Lake

İzmir

Afyon

Karabel

Beycesultan

L. Eğridir

İlgin

Ephesus (Apasas?)

L. Beyşehir

Büyük Menderes

Aphrodisias

Fassılar

Konya

Miletus

L. Burdur

Eflatun
Pınar

Karahüyük

Iasos

Hacılar

Çatal H

Müsgebi

Can Hasan

Antalya

Rhodes

Cypru

HITTITE AND OTHER ANCIENT SITES
IN ANATOLIA